FROM THE THRESHOLD OF HEAVEN

A Devotional Study in Advent and Lent

Martin A. Recio

Copyright © 2008 by Martin A. Recio

From The Threshold Of Heaven
A Devotional Study in Advent and Lent
by Martin A. Recio

Printed in the United States of America

ISBN 978-1-60647-204-0

All rights reserved solely by the author. The author guarantees all contents are original and do not infringe upon the legal rights of any other person or work. No part of this book may be reproduced in any form without the permission of the author. The views expressed in this book are not necessarily those of the publisher.

Unless otherwise indicated, Bible quotations are taken from The King James Version of the Bible, and The Revised Standard Version (RSV) of the Bible, Copyright © 1946, 1952, 1972 by the Division of Christian Education of the National Council of Churches of Christ in the U.S.A., Used by permission.

TXu 239-310, TXu 239-311, TXu 239-312, TXu 239-313, 1986.

www.xulonpress.com

Dedicated to my beloved wife, Lorene Ada Batchelor Recio

PREFACE

Of all the seasons of the Church year, no seasons speak to the human heart as do those of Advent and Lent. Advent speaks to the soul's expectation of the Savior's coming, while lent is a manifestation of his mission and self-sacrifice. Advent begins the incredible interlude of the Mighty God come in human form to dwell among the people of earth. The Holy Spirit overshadows this grand event, and tunes our hearts to the spiritual aura of the advent season.

Lent begins on Ash Wednesday and moves through the mystery of godliness. Tragedy is inherent in the season of lent. There is the betrayal by Judas, the trial before Pilate, and finally the crucifixion. But the good news of Easter morning came before the breaking of the day: "He is not here, but risen, even as he had said." Our faith emerged creative, redemptive and heroic: We have a Living and Risen Savior.

TABLE OF CONTENTS

FIRST ORDER OF ADVENT

1. First Sunday in Advent ....THE ANNUNCIATION OF JESUS
Mary's Response 16
God's Blessing on Those Who Hear 19

2. Second Sunday in Advent ....THE EXPECTANCY OF ADVENT
Advent Brings Renewal 23
Advent Comes With Gentle Strength..23

3. Third Sunday in Advent ....SHEPHERDS AND WISE MEN
Before Revelation, We had Only a Promise 26
The Reality of the Promise 26
Fulfillment..28

4. Fourth Sunday in Advent .... FROM THE THRESHOLD OF HEAVEN
From The Threshold of Heaven 31
Crossing the Human Threshold 32
Reaching Our Own Threshold 34

5. Christmas .... A STILLNESS
UNTO GOD
The Marvel of Birth 38
The Wonder of the Spirit...39
The Marvelous Gift of Faith 40

FIRST ORDER OF LENT

6. Ash Wednesday ....SPIRIT AND SOUL
AND BODY
Crossing the Jordan...44
Sanctified Wholly..45
God's Working 46

7. First Sunday in Lent..LENT AND
FAMILY VALUES
The Promise 50
The Holy Spirit and Family Values...............................51
The Reality of the Promise 51

8. Second Sunday in Lent ....FAITH IN
THINGS UNSEEN
We do not Lose Heart..53
When the Weight of Grief is Overbearing 55
When Death may Come 56

9. Third Sunday in Lent ....THE HEALING
WATERS OF LENT
What are the Symptoms?..60
The Healing Waters of Lent..61

From The Threshold Of Heaven

10. <u>Fourth Sunday in Lent</u> .... THEY HAD BEEN WITH JESUS
Turning Aside 64
God Responds 64
They Had Been With Jesus 65

11. <u>Passion Sunday</u> .... ON A DESERT ROAD
On a Desert Road 70
Our Lord's Passion 71
His Passion Has Meaning for Us 72

12. <u>Palm Sunday</u> .... IF THESE BE SILENT
An Enthusiastic Acclaim 75
Their Ardor Faded Away 77
Rejected of Men 78

13. <u>Maundy Thursday</u> .... THIS IS MY BODY
The Savior's Conception of The Last Supper 82
The Impact of the Sacrament on the Disciples 84
The Meaning of Maundy Communion for Us 85

14. <u>Good Friday</u> .... RECKONED WITH THE TRANSGRESSORS
The Issues of Life Spring From the Heart 88
The Intent of the Religious Authorities 89
Grace Greater Than All Our Sins 91

15. <u>Easter Sunday</u> .... ON THE FIRST DAY OF THE WEEK
The Story 93
At the Early Dawn 93
The Stone Was Rolled Away 94
Why do You Seek the Living Among the Dead 95
On The First Day of he Week 97

xi

KINGDOM TIDE INTERLUDE

16. THE MONUMENTAL MEANING 99

17. THE MAJESTY OF THE AWAKENING CHRIST 105
The Calm, the Storm, the Peace 106
Christ is All in All 108
The Majesty of the Awakening Christ 109

18. GOD WHO MADE THE WORLDS 111
What Is God Like? 112
The Nature of God's Dealings With Men 113
The Nature of Believing 114
God's Gift of Righteousness 115

THE SECOND ORDER OF ADVENT

19. First Sunday in Advent .... ADVENT PAST
God's Righteousness 120
Advent Past is not all Past 121

20. Second Sunday in Advent .... ADVENT PRESENT
The Present Age 123
Loss of Awareness 125
Advent Present 126

21. Third Sunday in Advent .... ADVENT FUTURE
Advent Brings Hope 128
The Spiritual Aura and Force of Advent 129
Advent Looks to the Future 130

22. Fourth Sunday in Advent ....THE MIRACLE
OF ADVENT
You Always Pray for a Miracle...
Advent Brings the Savior Near..135
Advent is a Time for Prayer...136

23. Christmas ....THIS WILL BE
A SIGN FOR YOU
The Situation...139
News From Angels..140
This Will be a Sign for You...141
The Wonder of it...142

THE SECOND ORDER OF LENT

24. Ash Wednesday ....SEEKING THE PRESENCE
The Estrangement Begins From the Heart...............................147
The Spirit of Lent Fills the Longing of the Soul......................148

25. First Sunday in Lent..............................FORESHADOWING
THE RESURRECTION
Only Believe 153
A Prelude to the Resurrection 153

26. Second Sunday in Lent ....THE PRELUDE OF
HUMILITY AND GLORY
God Does Not Work Through Overbearing Individuals..............156
When we are Unassuming, God Works 157
God Has Exalted Him 158

27. Third Sunday in Lent .... THIRTY PIECES OF SILVER
Analysis of the Transaction...162
Analysis of Judas Iscariot 163
The Transaction and the Individual...164

28. Fourth Sunday in Lent ....MY TIMES ARE
                                                IN GOD'S HANDS
My Time, God's Time 166
Our Lord's time, Our Time 168

29. Passion Sunday .... THE CROSS
                                                AND THE CROWN
The Cross and the Crown..172
The Cross and Crown in Human lives 172
Our Cross, Our Crown 174

30. Palm Sunday .... REJECTING
                                                   AND RECEIVING
Jesus Was Rejected Then 178
He is Rejected today 179
Christ Can Always be Received.................................181

31. Maundy Thursday ....I HAVE
                                                   PRAYED FOR YOU
I have Prayed for You..184
I Will Not Leave You Desolate 186
I Will Send The Counselor..187

32. Good Friday ....NE PLUS ULTRA
He Had Done No Wrong...190
Who Has Believed Our Report? 191
Ne Plus Ultra..193

33. Easter Sunday..........................SUNSET—SUNRISE
A Risen and Living Lord...195
Sunset—Sunrise 197
Sunrise, Heroic Optimism..198

FIRST ORDER OF ADVENT

CHAPTER 1

THE ANNUNCIATION OF JESUS

First Sunday in Advent.

For a people whose days were like the shadows that declined with the coming evening, and on whose lips the breath of life was stayed, the long years of dreaming, hoping, and waiting were over. They had looked to the Temple, to their service of worship, and even towards the heavens for some signs of the times. Their holy men had spoken of the grace that should come to them:

> Searching what, or what manner of time the Spirit of Christ, which was in them did signify when it testified before hand of the sufferings of Christ, and the glory that should follow. (l Peter 1:11)

The proclamation, when it came was one of consolation, the comforting annunciation of the coming Redeemer, promised of God ages ago through his prophets. The good news came through the appearance of a ministering angel. His presence shone at the nature of his calling and the longed for substance of his message. The heavenly messenger brought to a world confused in darkness and gripped in despair, the joy of their near deliverance. The fulfillment of the promise was delivered in tidings of peace and reconciliation, embodied in the birth of the holy child, the baby Jesus. He would be called the Son of God. And he came not only as the hope of Israel, but also as the crown jewel of the Father's gifts of grace. He came as the consummation of all the prophets, priests, and kings God had given the nation. He came as the beginning and end of God's creation. He would make a way for the redeemed of the Lord to pass through the veil and into the presence of the Eternal.

St. Luke wrote that it was a time when the Holy Spirit overshadowed the land, when God sent the angel Gabriel to the city of Nazareth. The angelic messenger came to a virgin espoused to a man named Joseph, of David's lineage. Her name was Mary. The angel's first words were startling.

She was troubled in her mind and wondered what sort of greeting this might be. She also wondered if it might not be a vision. She had heard about the visions which came to the ancient ones. But the angel immediately added.

> Fear not Marry, for thou hast found favour with God. And, behold, thou shalt conceive in thy womb and bring forth a son, and thou shalt call his name Jesus...He shall be great, and shall be called the Son of the Highest: and the Lord God shall give unto him the throne of his father David: and he will reign over the house of Jacob for ever. (Luke 1:30-33)

Mary asked how can these things be, seeing that I know not a man? And the angel replied.

> The Holy Ghost shall come upon thee, and the power of the Highest shall overshadow thee: therefore also that thing which shall be born of thee shall be called the Son of God. (Luke 1:38)

Mary's Response.

This is the first Sunday in advent. Advent means the coming of the baby Jesus. We look to the incredible interlude of the Son of God come to earth in human form. God sent the angel of his presence, Gabriel, to make the annunciation of the holy birth. Although Mary was startled by the initial greeting, "Hail, thou art highly favored," the details of the child's person filled her with wonder. She knew that the coming one would be, and do, all that Moses had written in the law and the prophets. And who among us would not have been startled at such a greeting? And who would not have wondered about its meaning?

When he grew to manhood, this holy thing born of her would be worthy to open the book of the seven seals. He would declare unto men the councils of God, and to extend to all the consolation of his redemption. Mary expressed this in her hymn of gratitude. This was a revelation of the Father's mercy, an outpouring of grace in the Spirit and power of the Most High. In the simplicity of his grace, in dealing with men, God confounds those wise in their own eyes by the simplicity of the means used to fulfill his promises. The good tidings did not come in the grandeur of the temple, or before the golden altar of incense, and not even within the porch of the sanctuary. The heavenly encounter took place in a quiet, humble home of Nazareth, amidst deep human lowliness. And even the Son, in adult life, teaching about the Kingdom of heaven, would be characterized as meek and lowly in heart.

In revealing the birth of the holy child, the angel Gabriel told of his greatness: his name would be Jesus, he would be acknowledged as the Son of God, fulfill the people's spiritual longing, and be given a never ending kingdom.

Had the news come to the religious authorities, would they have believed? Did they not reject him, and crucify him in disdain and unbelief? Surely, the Lord God must have known. Mary, however, through a living faith and devotion to the kingdom of God, was a vessel prepared unto honor. In a humble voice, she responded, "Let be unto me according to the word of the Lord."

Although the name Jesus means he who will save his people, his conception caused Mary a problem. And yet faith in the power of God can always cause problems to be resolved—according to his purpose. When Mary was found to be with child, Joseph thought to put her away quietly. He wanted to avoid the possibility of disgrace over a conception not the product of a lawful marriage. But is it not written, "The Lord knows who are his?" Joseph's mind scarcely turned on these things, when an angel of the Lord appeared to him in a dream, and said.

> Joseph, thou son of David, fear not to take unto thee Mary thy wife: for that which is conceived in her is of the Holy Ghost.
> And she shall bring forth a son, and thou shalt call his name JESUS: for he shall save his people from their sins.
> (Matt 1:20-21)

The ministering angel brought assurance to Joseph with his message. And realizing it was a communication from God, Joseph drove all doubts from his mind. Being a man of the kingdom, he complied with the request and did as the angel instructed him. Like his wife, Mary, he displayed a heart willingness to be of service for the grace of God—and for the glory of the kingdom of heaven. God works through men and women, bringing his will to pass through those who respond to his call to service. And however humble or small the service may seem, it is still a contribution to the mission of the church. Mary gave her life for the onward movement of God's purpose, and was endowed with the impulse of the Holy Spirit. Under the Spirit's leading, her own spirit issued forth in a Psalm of gratitude and praise.

> My soul magnifies the Lord, and my spirit rejoices in God my Savior, for he has regarded the low estate of his handmaiden. For behold, henceforth all generations will call me blessed; for he who is mighty has done great things for me, and holy is his name...He has helped his servant Israel, in remembrance of his mercy, as he spoke to our fathers, to Abraham and to his posterity for ever.
> (Luke 1:46-45)

There followed a sequence to the annunciation of the birth of the baby Jesus. One humble person willing to be used for God's service, and the promise made to the fathers about the coming Savior is fulfilled. One maid surrendering to God's grace, and grace is extended to the entire human race, and extended for ever. One humble woman responded to the words of the angel, and the whole world benefited. Of this we can be certain, to those who love God and are called according to his purpose, in their own appointed time, the summons will come; and the work of some aspect of the kingdom will depend on their response.

God's Blessing on Those Who Would Hear.

It was true then, and true today, with a call to service, God extends the promise of his presence and blessing. The word to Mary was, "The Holy spirit will come upon you; and the power of the Most High will overshadow you." Yet, the actual realization of the great things that were to occur through the birth of the holy child, was not so much what Mary would do, but what God would do through her. Because Mary responded for God's service, his presence and power insured the outcome of the things told her. She affirmed that God vindicated the words spoken to the fathers. She understood that a willingness to be of service would be followed by an outpouring of God's providence.

Those aware of the things which this season commemorates can respond to the summons of God's Spirit, and they can look forward to that more perfect day. The advent season is full of busy noises, of bells, lights, and decorated trees.

But there may be a moment when the Spirit of the Most High breaks a silence through it all, and he will come near. Like the winds coming from the four corners of the earth, he seeks lodging in the hearts of men, women, and little children. Like Mary, the handmaiden of the Lord, let it be to each of us according to the word of the Lord. According to the voice of the angel and the impulse of the Spirit, so let it be to all of us during this advent season. Then, like Mary, our souls will magnify the Lord, and our spirits will rejoice in God our Savior. For he who is mighty has done great things; he has blessed us with mercy, even unto us, and to our posterity for ever.

CHAPTER 2

THE EXPECTANCY OF ADVENT

Second Sunday in Advent.

As we move into the Christmas season, the memories of the past, and the expectations of the future are brought into focus. We recall the story of the shepherds passing the night in the fields, watching over their flocks. There was the sudden appearing of the angel which startled them. And although fearful, they were wide awake with anticipation, listening to the news given them by the ministering messenger. When the angel had gone, the shepherds wondered about what they had heard, talked about it, and resolved to act. And with haste they made their way to the city of Bethlehem.

The Ravages of Time.

We had built a new church in the town of Lewiston, California. It was in response to the large growth of population that came into the valley to work on the Trinity Dam Project. The architectural design, an A-frame structure with redwood siding and multicolored glass windows on the south side, blended in beautifully with the surrounding wooded mountains and the snow-capped Trinity Alps. It was an attractive building. The interior of the sanctuary was conducive to worship.

But when I visited the valley again, nearly forty years later, the devastation of the years had been cruel. Apparently it had received little care. The color of the redwood siding had faded; windows were cracked, broken, and covered with cardboard. The large redwood cross was gone, and the once impressive architectural structure had become little more than a derelict. When no care is taken, time can be destructive.

With us, the passage of years has also taken its toll, and our sense of higher things may have grown dim. The duties of daily life and our struggle to keep our world intact have drained us physically, mentally, and emotionally. Rest and recreation will restore our mental and physical vigor. But there is a deep stirring within. Depleted, we long for that moment when we shall feel the healing presence of grace. And as we think on these things, the memories of the past are awakened.

The story of the shepherds in the field, waiting for the coming of day, comes to us from the far distant pass. Yet it evokes memories of the Christmas seasons we have known when we were children; and for some of us that may have been ages ago. We remember the occasion when we gathered with friends, family, and loved ones, when our hearts sang with gladness. We remember the faces, smiles, and the incidents that brought laughter. We remember that certain way each had of doing things and the gesture of love that made them dear to us. And as we come to the gathering again, we look forward to it with joy.

This year the circle has grown smaller, and also larger. Old friends and loved ones have gone on. Grandchildren have arisen to take their place in the family circle. Of those that have gone, their memories linger in our minds, and we cherish the thought of them. Every one has grown older. A touch of gray lines our hair and our physical strength is not what it once was. We know that the things of this world do not last for ever. Those things that endure the ravages of time, we believe, are of a spiritual nature—the things that hover unseen over the physical world. We sense it in the aura that comes with these festive days. It comes like a soft wind that awakens the thoughts of the mind and touches the soul. From these memories we garner strength for today, and for tomorrow, and for the day after that. This season tells us that time does not take everything.

The Expectancy of Advent Brings Renewal.

Not only the memories of the past, but also the expectations of the future are aroused by the Christmas season. We look for the signs of the times as the day approaches, because advent involves waiting; and this waiting is with expectation. The heart of the matter is that the expectancy of advent brings renewal. To renew means to make as if new again, or to make fresh and strong once more. It means to rekindle hope and restore vigor to the life of the soul. In advent, we seek regeneration.

To every Sunday worship service we come as they came of old, looking for a hand to hold amidst the shadows of the evening. We come seeking him who can respond to the pressing needs of the soul. We come for a voice that speaks to our sorrows and to our loss of the past. We unite in worship for a vision of higher things that can refresh the inner life. We seek like Aaron and Moses to stand within the holy place, and to abide for a time under the wings of The Almighty. We come longing for that touch of grace that can assure us that God has heard our prayers and accepted our worship.

We wait and hope, and more often than not, by hope we are saved. Twenty, fourteen, ten more days before Christmas. The days are marked off on our calendar. And as the time draws nearer, we feel the increase sense of the movment of things unseen. There is a silence that portends the doing of great things; of wonder, of heavenly hosts, and of angel visitants. We look for the glory of the Lord, and for the grace that was revealed to men on earth. We are assured that if we wait with expectancy, God's presence will make itself known. Advent brings renewal of heart, mind, and soul to those who have confessed the Lord Jesus.

Advent Comes With Gentle Strength.

The Spirit that moves through the advent season can also touch our lives. When we confess our need, the Savior responds with power, for advent comes with gentle strength. The Lord, "He gives power to the faint, and to him who has no might, he increases strength" (Isaiah 40:28). For the ware, tare, and stress which this season brings, we all need added strength. Strength is the quality of being strong; it means new force, vigor, and durability. It comes with power to resist the strain that these busy days will demand from us. When we say that advent comes with gentle strength, we mean strength grown tender, that is considerate, kind, and gracious. And as we look to him, surely the Lord will renew our strength, because the expectancy of our religious beliefs is embodied in Christ our Lord.

Indeed, advent tells us that the eternal promises were fulfilled, and fulfilled beyond all human expectations. The memories of the past, and our hopes for the future are made clear once again. The Savior who was once a child is with us today as the exalted Lord of heaven and earth. Moreover, he has promised to be with us for all the years that remain to us on earth. For all that may lie in the future, he will be there to fulfill his promises of strength and renewal. Even now, as the day approaches, he comes to seal us with his Spirit and to hold us for his own; for the past with all its glad memories, for the present with all its expectations, and for the future with all that it may bring.

CHAPTER 3

SHEPHERDS AND WISE MEN

Third Sunday in Advent.

Orbiting the earth, the Hubble Space Telescope is pointed to the far reaches of the universe, obtaining light from quasars and star clouds millions of light years away. Through its observation, astronomers are attempting to gather information about interstellar gas clouds, dark matter, black holes, and mass. What are they looking for? They are seeking knowledge about the origins of the universe. They are looking for a revelation that will shed light on the mystery of existence. In this age of scientific wonder, we do not think it unreasonable to conceive of the universe as created with intelligent purpose and design; or to retain the thought in this advent season, that *"Through faith we understand that the worlds were framed by the word of God, so that the things which are seen were not made of things which do appear (Hebrews 11:3).*

What do the observations of the Space Telescope reveal? They will reveal only more wonders and new island universes of God's creation. Surely the one to whom we look, and worship, as the ultimate creator, was never one to fear the mysteries unfolded by the shedding of new light.

There was a man in Jerusalem whose name was Simeon. Scripture states that the Holy Spirit was upon him, and that it had been revealed to him that he should not see death before he had seen the Lord's Christ. When Simeon saw the child Jesus in the Temple, his words gave expression to the thoughts that had given an impulse to his life for so many years.

> Lord, now lettest thou thy servant depart in peace according to thy word; for mine eyes have seen thy salvation which thou hast prepared in the presence of all the people, a light for revelation to the Gentiles. (Luke 2:29-32)

Even in the advent season we still need the revelation of God's grace to guide us; and we need it whether it be an angel visitant or a guiding star. And how true it is, the fault lies not in our stars, but in us.

Before Revelation, We had Only a Promise.

In the beginning God created the heavens and the earth, and the earth was waste and void; and darkness was on the face of the deep. Before revelation we had but a promise; but then a promise is the basis of hope and expectation. Mary, in her Psalm of praise, recalled that God helped his people, when he remembered the word spoken to the fathers. As the eternal Spirit moved over the face of the waters, God said, let there be light; and a new way of hope emerged for the human race in the promise of the coming Redeemer. The darkness which had fallen on our progenitors in Paradise was driven back.

On that occasion in the Temple, Simeons's faith was burning brightly. He was always righteous and devout, looking for the advent of the consolation of Israel. Attentive to the movement of things unseen, he was at worship when the parents of the child brought the baby Jesus to the Temple. Taking the child in his arms, Simeon blessed and praised God through the words which he had spoken. He held the promised one in his arms.

The Reality of the Promise.

Advent brought reality to the promise, for the days preceding the Savior's coming were a time of signs and wonders. The Shepherds saw an angel and the multitude of the heaven hosts, while the Wise Men saw the natal star that shone with glory. We wonder whether the glory of the Lord will ever shine round about us, as it did to those watchful keepers of the sheep. The nations or the earth are still filled with misgivings and under the fear of the atom. We are appalled at the vastness of space and the expanding universe. Rockets and nuclear warheads have been produced in such vast numbers, that if unleashed, darkness will again cover the face of the earth. For over sixty years, only the possibility of mutual extinction compelled the nations to seek peace. But in heralding advent, the angel said, "Fear not," the tidings are of great joy. In advent, God penetrated and drove pack the darkness. He brought peace and good will to men.

The Wise Men who came from the East wanted a clearer vision of God, they wanted a God who loved and cared. They came seeking more than understanding. They came looking for him who was a child, and yet born a King.

Although wise, these men knew that no human being could lift the veil of the Kingdom of righteousness and peace. In the Christ child, the Wise Men looked towards that spiritual realm, where fear was banished and death but a transition to a higher land. They needed a light for revelation, and in God's time, the sign appeared. It must have shown like the bright and morning star. And when they saw it, though already old, they mounted up as on the wings of an eagle, and followed the star. To those who look to the heavens, who long for a clearer vision of God, the revelations will come. And revelation is always a lifting of the veil, a shedding of light and knowledge of that which was once hidden and obscure.

There, in Bethlehem, the curtain ascended softly, in the quiet of the evening. In the valley of Judea, in the plains of the east, and in our own time and place, the veil will be lifted, and the Lord will reveal himself. And to each, the experience will be unique. While the shepherds had only to watch and wait, the Wise Men had to travel, seek, and search for the unveiling of the mystery. But whether we watch and wait in anticipation, or are moved to seek and search, the advent of the holy child will be as the Lord of heaven and earth, and Savior of the world. With the Lord God, it is always this way, for with God a promise is as good as done. Advent brought fulfillment of God's word; and it came with a gift of faith, and with a light for revelation to the Gentiles.

Fulfillment.

In these days when we remember the anniversary of our Lord's first appearing, the season is filled with meaning for the men and women of our time. We are never beyond the need for more knowledge about God's grace and purpose. Time and place are of no consequences. The Spirit which revealed the good tidings to the shepherds and Wise Men, still moves over the broad reaches of the land. The Savior's coming is with love and grace, creating a fellowship of peace and harmony. We acknowledge our need for guidance and revelation, because the people of the space age are no different inwardly from those of past generations. Among us we still have the troubled in heart, the despairing, and those seeking the peace of God's forgiveness. We wait for the soft lifting of the veil, where the inner sanctuary of the holy place will be revealed, where we may experience the nearness of the presence of God. We wait for the coming of the Spirit in power to comfort and guide.

The wonder of advent will remain with us always, for its movement can be felt in the soul—for Christ is present in the quiet of the evening, and where two or three are gathered in his name. The Spirit responds to the prayer of the child, and to the praise of the elder. Our Lord comes to the large cities, to the country villages, and to the humble homes of those who seek. And all the while, to the penitent, the absolution of God's mercy is graciously given. Advent brings consolation and peace. This is the message which we have proclaimed; and from the glory which he had with the father, the Lord Jesus came as a light for revelation to the Gentiles.

Shepherds, in the fields abiding,
Watching o're your flocks by night,
God with man is now residing.
Yonder shines the infant light.

From The Threshold Of Heaven

Sages, leave your contemplations,
Brighter visions beam afar:
Seek the great Desire of nations,
You have seen his natal star:

Saints before the altar bending,
Watching long in hope and fear,
Suddenly the Lord, descending,
In his temple shall appear. (James Montgomery)

CHAPTER IV

FROM THE THRESHOLD OF HEAVEN

Fourth Sunday in Advent.

In the city of David, devout souls in the first advent season still retained in their hearts one hope, that of the coming Redeemer. It was the consolation of Israel viewed through the prophetic future. The people had the Temple, their central place of their worship. It spoke of the past, when God had worked wonders with his people. As the Temple related to their religion, there was only one real Temple, the Temple in Jerusalem. It spoke of God's presence, the dwelling place of the Most High. This was the only sanctuary in which the God-accepted priesthood offered sacrifice. Here, in the Temple stood the Ark, containing the Tablets of the Law, the Shewbread, and Aaron's rod that once budded. Then too, here the incense rose heavenward from the Golden Altar, as the symbol that God had accepted their worship and prayers. Here, also, was kept the seven-branched candlestick indicative of God's presence.

From The Threshold of Heaven.

The Temple service and all its symbols pointed to a bright future. That future was the coming of the kingdom of heaven, wherein was found righteousness, peace, and joy in the Holy Spirit. Its essence looked to the inner, spiritual life given to men by the coming of the anointed one. The advent season looks to the time when the promised one came from the threshold of heaven to inhabit a body like ours. For this giving of grace, the world waited. God's visitation always comes when most needed. Today the times become full once again, as grace moves through this season. It falls like the gentle drops of dew upon those who seek, awakening the life of the soul.

Crossing the Human Threshold.

When the holy infant crossed the human threshold, he became identified with the human race. "Blessed be the Lord God of Israel," said Zacarhias, "for he has visited and redeemed his people" (Luke 1:68). Though he came by way of a manger, the Lord Jesus came to visit and to redeem. It was not a fleeting thing, but a visitation that had the imprint of eternity. His presence remains and continues with us. His birth gave a new beginning for the human race, as every threshold is a point of beginning. Having become a part of our personal experience, and having moved our souls, it was never our Redeemer's intent to vanish and flee away. His word to us was: "I will be with you always."

Still, the temple of his dwelling place would no longer be a sanctuary created of stone, but of flesh and blood. His presence would no longer be attested to by the golden alter of incense and the seven-branched candlestick, but by the Spirit residing in humble souls and contrite hearts. And the wonder of his grace is this; that whenever the Savior crosses a human threshold, it is always a redeeming experience. Whether the crossing be during the advent season, or in the following Christmastide, the Lord comes to abide. It is his abiding with us that awakens the heart strings of our souls, quickens our faith, and causes the conscious acceptance of his grace. His words come to us as though carried on the wings of ministering spirits.

Abide in me, and I in you. As the branch cannot bear fruit of itself, except it abide in the vine: no more will you, except you abide in me. (John 15:14)

Yet, who can abide the day of his coming? And who shall stand when he appeareth? Because he came with mercy and grace, and covered us over with his righteousness, we all can abide the day of his coming. And is it not true that we pray for the reality of our Savior's presence?

Abide with me, fast falls the evening tide;
The darkness deepens, Lord with me abide.
When other helpers fail and comforts flee
O thou who changes not, abide with me.
(Henry Lyte, 1847)

What happens when the Savior comes to stay? He brings assurance, a feeling of confidence and security. With many, there is a groping, a misdirected searching after an assurance of faith. At times, our hold on spiritual things is tenuous. It seems to hang by a slender thread. But when Christ draws near, the doubts vanish. A quiet fullness takes possession of us, and confidence is restored. Concerning our faith, we will have gained a deeper feeling of security and peace. While the advent of our Redeemer has not yet brought peace throughout the world, he does bring peace of mind and tranquility of soul to believing hearts. And peace is a tonic word. It has the overtones of inner healing.

When we speak about the peace that our Lord brings, we have in mind freedom from internal strife, an undisturbed state of the soul, where there is an absence of spiritual conflict. When Christ abides with us, there is serenity, a calm and quiet that stills the troubled heart. And the advent season comes with our Savior's words of invitation: "You believe in God, believe also in me" (John 14:11). Yet, unless we invite him to abide with us, our Lord can do none of these things. We must also abide in him, "as the branch cannot bear fruit of itself."

And herein lies the manifestation of the Kingdom of heaven, wherein dwelleth righteousness, peace, and joy in the Holy Spirit.

Reaching Our Own Threshold.

When the advent message came to the Virgin Mary, she responded: "Let it be unto me according to thy word." When the shepherds heard the voice of the angels, with wonder in their hearts, they said, "Let us go even now and see this thing which the Lord has made known to us." When the Wise Men from the East saw the star, they rejoiced, and awakened with a new born hope, they followed it to him whom their hearts desired. The individual, the human soul, has a threshold of realization. It is the point at which one awakens with a response.

For many, the threshold of realization to spiritual things is difficult to arouse. The world has imposed on them a dull insensitivity to the person of Christ—and to his claim upon the human heart. But unless we come to the threshold of realization, to the point at which we awaken to the message of the season, peace and joy in the Holy Spirit will never come upon us. In advent, it is wise to be spiritually sensitive to the signs of the times.

When Elijah stood in the cleft of the rock, waiting for the visitation of the Lord God, there came a mighty wind, roaring in all its fury, but God was not in the whirlwind. Then came the earthquake, shaking the earth to its foundation, but God was not in the earthquake. Then came the fire consuming all in its path, but again, God was not in the fire. Finally, there occurred the gentle stilling of the elements, the calming of the tempest—and the elements were at peace. In the midst of this serenity and tranquility, Elijah heard the calling of the Spirit. It came to him like a still, small voice. For this Elijah had been waiting. He had reached the point of awareness, and his soul awakened in recognition. He responded. He knelt and worshipped, covering his face with his mantle. He stood in the presence of The Almighty.

Mary, the shepherds, the Wise Men, and Elijah all awoke to the touch of the Spirit. In this advent season, what will it take to arouse the sensitivity of our soul to spiritual things? The presence of the Spirit is seeking to reveal the glory of the Lord. He seeks to reach us with the glad tidings of the Savior's coming. He strives to bring us to the moment of realization, to lead us to an awareness of the abiding presence. The main question is what will it take to evoke a response in our hearts? And, would we be willing to abide the moment of the Savior's coming into our lives? Will we receive the love and grace that he brings? And will we accept his invitation? Have we forgotten, "God has visited and redeemed his people?"

To redeem means to ransom and rescue. To redeem means to fulfill the promise symbolized in the Temple worship service—God's promise to deliver his people from sin and its consequences. Though many will not hear the message of the herald angels, nor see the glory of the natal star, we ought not to be insensitive to the Savior's appearing. The many things that we must do during this season ought not to obscure our vision. His words of invitation reveal the simplicity and sincerity of his grace: "You believe in God, believe also in me." And if you do this: believe in him, the Lord Jesus will cross the threshold of your heart. He will visit you, and redeem your soul for his Kingdom, and he will abide with you for ever.

CHAPTER 5

A STILLNESS UNTO GOD
(Christmas)

In his Illustrated History of The Second World War, Winston Churchill wrote, "The First World War was a conflict in which, for the first time in modern history, the entire life-blood and energy of nations were poured out in the field of battle in wrath and slaughter." But on Christmas day, for a few hours, the entire western front grew quiet. It were as though the men who had been trying to destroy each other a short time before, came to recognize the significance of this day—which ought to have been celebrated in thought of peace and good will. They came up out of the trenches, came together, and for a few brief hours, greeted each other and exchanged gifts. And though hostilities resumed later on, for a brief span of time, the meaningful impact of Christmas day could not be overlooked.

When angels sang and a star traversed the skies, when shepherds watched and Wise Men marveled, God sent forth his Son. It was in the days when Caesar Augustus levied the tax, when the whole world was ruled from Rome, and when each came to his own city to be enrolled. It was the time of which the prophets had spoken, and of which old men had seen visions. Snow covered Mount Hermon, King Herod reigned in Jerusalem, and all the inns were filled. Joseph went from Galilee to the city of David in accordance with the imperial decree. And while he was there, Mary, his wife, gave birth to the holy child. The birth of this one child, and the whole human race rejoiced with an exceedingly great rejoicing.

The Marvel of Birth.

Although the angel of the annunciation revealed the character and mission of the baby Jesus, not everything about the nature of the average child is revealed, when he becomes a living soul. At birth, Charles Dickens, author of Barnaby Rudge, The Tale of Two Cities, A Christmas Carol, and many other novels, was small, sickly, and appeared under nourished. His father thought he would not live to maturity. Fortunately, he was wrong. The birth of every child is a wonderful, marvelous event; and with watch and care, the child can develop the possibilities and potentialities inherent in his life.

On Christmas day we celebrate the birth of the baby Jesus. It reminds us of bells and stars, of shepherds and wise men, of the inn and the manger, and of the bright eyes of little children. The child asleep on a bed of straw in the manger embodied the hopes of Israel and the aspirations of the prophets. And yet, are not our hopes and fears centered on every newborn child brought into the family? We see visions and dream dreams of his future, we pray for the safety of the child, and hope he will grow with a sound mind and body. And all the while, we wait and watch, as the miracle of growth takes place. So it was with the baby Jesus born in the manger. Yet, it was not until the shepherds came, told their story, and the wise men brought gifts that worship and adoration came to the holy child.

The shepherds came to worship, when they knelt before him whom the angels had made known to them. In bringing their gifts, the wise men paid him homage. In our times, we worship because the Son of God was given, and because the glory of the Lord assumed human form. We pay homage, because like the shepherds, we know what the Savior came to do—that from the beginning, Jesus came to give his life as a ransom for sin and to reconcile us to the Father. The wise men may not have known that the manger envisioned a cross, or that the baby in the manger would later be characterized as the Lamb of God who takes away the sins of the world. They came to worship him born king of the Jews. But the men of the fields and keepers of sheep knew that in the city of David was born to them a Savior who was Christ the Lord. This revelation came in the message of the angel. Born a Savior, that was the wonder of the holy birth. Scarcely had they heard the message, when they came in haste. And they made known the sayings which had been told them concerning the baby Jesus; and it is narrated that all who heard it marveled at what the shepherds had told them. Mary, the mother, however, kept and pondered all these things in her heart, like a stillness unto God.

The Wonder of the Spirit.

When Mary received the words of the annunciation from the angel, she wondered how all these things could possibly be. The heavenly messenger said, "The Holy Spirit shall come upon thee, and the power of the Most High will overshadow thee." Though born among the humblest of circumstances, the birth of the baby Jesus came as the work of the Spirit of God. This was the real miracle attendant upon the Savior's birth—the manifestation of the Holy Spirit, the Lord and Giver of life, and who had spoken through the prophets. Bound in the Savior's birth was the foreshadowing of the inner, spiritual life he would bring to his people: the first Adam became a living being, but the Second Adam became a life giving Spirit.

What is that can change one's nature, soften the disposition of the heart, alter the attitude of the mind, and make him aware of deep inner realities. Difficulties alone cannot do this, nor will pain, nor time. The change must be effected by something so moving, that it touches the soul. Asleep in the manger, the infant Redeemer may not have appeared as the Son of God whose eyes were like a flame of fire, and whose feet were like burnished bronze. But on the day of Pentecost, the power of the Spirit was revealed, and those upon whom it fell and were so endowed, seemed to have spoken with the voice of men and angels. The birth of the Christ child began the era of the reign of the Spirit in human souls; and where nurtured, there the rule of the Kingdom of heaven begins for that life. We feel the reality of this marvelous working in the mysterious quickening power that moves through this season, the presence of which everywhere is sensed.

The Marvelous Gift of Faith.

"Marvel not," said our Lord to his disciples, to Nicodemus, and to us today. The gifts of faith, and the promises, are to you and to your children forever. But unless we believe with a receptive heart, we will never share in the Kingdom of heaven. The Christmas promise comes with the birth of the holy child, the endowment of the Spirit, and the gift of faith. Yet, neither the Spirit, nor faith can come to us, unless we make room to receive them.

When the child was about to be delivered by Mary, they could find no room in which to lodge. Whether it was indifference on the part of the innkeeper, or the fact that the inn was too crowded with other guests, or that someone was indisposed to believe, the result was the same. No room was given for lodging to a mother about to give birth. That people of the day did not expect the holy family to come so near, nor did they receive them. For complete delivery of a gratuity, there must be an acceptance. To receive means to accept that which is offered, and to give admittance to. Unless we take the gift of God into possession, give room and admittance to the Savior as an indwelling guest, we will never know the reality of the promise.

In these days, the higher and unseen aspects of life may be crowded out of our thoughts by neglect, by other gifts, or by lack of expectation. Faith remains the substance of things hoped for. If we hope for it, we will wait with expectation to receive it. For millions throughout the years, since the stillness of that night in Bethlehem, the heavenly gifts have been offered and given. Though millions have come to receive the Savior's grace, the offer is always extended for those who seek and are ready to receive. The Lord God is able to multiply infinitely the dispensation of his love; and he can do so many times more than the stars in number. Thus, like Mary, we keep and ponder all these things in our hearts. Like the shepherds and wise men, we worship and adore the Lord Jesus. But our faith must be expectant, giving admittance to his Spirit. This is to experience the inner, deep reality of our religious beliefs. Nothing, then, shall ever more separate us from the love of God which is in Christ Jesus our Lord, whom the Father sent to the world from the threshold of heaven.

FIRST ORDER OF LENT

CHAPTER 6

ASH WEDNESDAY

SPIRIT AND SOUL AND BODY

Ash Wednesday is the point of beginning for the lenten season. It is followed by the four Sundays of lent; then come Passion Sunday and Palm Sunday; and within Holy Week, we have Maundy Thursday, Good Friday, and Easter Sunday. God has not given us the spirit of fear, but of power, of love, and of a sound mind. And we reason it is beneficial to know what we are about during these days, which along with advent, are the most significant weeks of the Christian year. We know instinctively that to avoid mere compliance with outward formality or with ritualistic observance, our hearts, souls, and minds must be affected. In so far as possible, we ought to move with the impulse of the Spirit during the lenten season.

We confess that we seek something divine and eternal in the meaning of the season of lent. We trust that within the providence of God's grace, a small measure of spiritual perception may come upon us. We pray the Father's kindness might touch our hearts, and that by this inner sense, we may be able to distinguish the divine aura and revelation from our own thoughts and conceptions. We trust that this will be so for all who have turned to the Lord Jesus, looking for a deeper understanding and fuller experience in the Kingdom of grace and glory.

In his letter to the Thessalonians, who had appealed to St. Paul for counsel and direction in their walk with the Lord, the apostle wrote them a concluding blessing.

> May the God of peace himself sanctify you wholly; and may your spirit and soul and body be kept sound and blameless at the coming of the Lord Jesus. He who calls you is faithful, and he will do it. (l Thess 5:23 RSV)

Crossing The Jordan.

Over across that river Jordan lay the land to which the people Israel were directed since first they were redeemed from the house of bondage and delivered from servitude in Egypt. They were brought this far by divine leading, intervention, and by works without number. In his kindness, God restored and refreshed them time and time again. In his goodness he fed them with manna; and in his providence he brought them through the wilderness as on eagle's wings. Repeatedly, as they settled in the land beyond the Jordan, and grew in wealth and population, they were reminded to think back on God's dealings with them, the redemption from captivity he had wrought, and to consecrate themselves to his service.

There were times when they wandered far from the paths of righteousness, when they forgot the nature of their calling, and neglected the worship of the one true God. This always occurs to a nation, or to a people individually, when they have prospered, obtained an abundance of possessions, and are counted members of an affluent society. We drift away from the sense of the presence of God. Though the body may do well, the spirit and soul become severely distressed. We sense a loss, a lack, and wonder whether we have missed the way of our eternal destiny. The coming of the holy seasons are precisely for these reasons, to make us aware once again, more deeply than at other times, of spiritual realities; of God's grace, of the Savior's love, and of our need to be brought near the cross.

The worship services, the symbols of our religion—like the bread and wine of Holy Communion, the dove, the lighting of the candles, and the up-lifted cross are meant to bring us to reflection on the goodness of God. We are led to think on his providence, his past and present dealings with us, that the spiritual impulse of our souls being awakened, we might seek the saving way of God's forgiveness. Ash Wednesday is the day of the year when we seek to cross over the Jordan into the land where Jesus walked. We will seek to clasp, as it were, his unseen hand, and travel together with our Lord along the road of our own spiritual Emmaus.

Sanctified Wholly.

Paul's instructions in righteousness are just as valid today, as they were for the ancient saints of Thessalonica. We ought always to exercise care for the welfare of our spirit, soul, and body. A disturbed internal disposition can have an adverse effect on our religious life, thought process, and perception of spiritual things. When our mental and emotional states are affected, the heart and soul are troubled. Our outward acts must be in conformity with our inner thoughts and impulses. Whether the touch of healing begins with the heart and soul, or with the mental process and emotions, God's grace upon our lives brings harmony to the inner and outer man. Our whole person is affected by our Lord's love and grace.

To sanctify means to consecrate for holy use; mentally, it means not to let the mind wander from God in its affection. Our movement toward this end begins with a penitent attitude, a receptive heart, and a willing mind to serve the Lord God. We look for the blessing of his grace in the season of lent; and this he is ever so ready to bestow on men and women who love his appearing. In our religious life we believe, receive, and respond as a total person. And when faith is born in us, it is always the result of the response of the heart, mind, and soul. Some thoughts must always fly before we believe, and we must be moved inwardly. Of one thing we are certain, when God's grace, amazing as it is, touches our hearts and awakens the life of the soul, the mental assent is sure to follow. Then we will have crossed over into that goodly land, the days of grace and glory, known as the Lenten season.

Although Ash Wednesday was so named because of the significance of ashes used by the penitent as a sign of humility and cleansing in their address to God, the meaning conveyed is true. Prayer and self-denial are always elements which manifest a desire for the revival of our religious life. It is a seeking for the higher plane, looking for the elevation of the soul in worship. And as we draw near his presence, we may be standing on holy ground; for holiness implies nearness to God. Is this not true? That what God would require of us, he bestows upon us in his grace.

God's Working.

How are we sanctified wholly? And how do our spirits, souls, and bodies become preserved blameless unto the day of Jesus Christ? Blameless means to have been found without significant fault or wrong. And yet, it is not our doing, but God's working. It is written that without righteousness—moral excellence—we cannot see God. The righteousness which we seek in the season of lent, and which is the end of self-denial, fasting, and prayer, is a saving gift of God's grace. It comes from God to all who acknowledge him as their heavenly Father and have turned to the Lord Jesus: "The righteousness of God, which is through faith in Christ Jesus" (Romans 3:22). And the beauty of it all is that it is apart from the law, that ancient schoolmaster.

For the believer, the penitent, and for all who would draw near the Father, righteousness is the inclination of the heart toward God—the affection of the mind that has turned to him, and the disposition of compliance to the divine direction for our lives: "To do justice, and to love kindness, and humbly walk with your God" (Micah 6:8).

Ash Wednesday begins our pilgrimage through the last days of the interlude of the Mighty God on earth. It is the commencement of our own road to Emmaus, where spiritual awakening occurred in the lives of those two travelers of long ago. Somewhere along our journey, we may sense the presence of The Eternal; and through the impulse of his Spirit, our hearts may be gently moved. Our souls will be awakened, and our spirits revived. What need we do? Simply walk with the Lord Jesus along the way.

Prayer.

Eternal God and gracious Father, as we come to the beginning of the new day, and into the season of grace and glory, we pray that thy Spirit may be upon us, may move us, and work in us thy holy will. Give us penitent hearts that we may rise above the obscurity of a busy world, and find him whom our hearts desire. Amen.

O Holy Spirit, cleanse the thoughts of our hearts, and redeem the imaginations of our minds, so that in coming to thee, throughout the Lenten season, we may find grace to help in time of need. We pray thee through Jesus Christ our Lord.
                    Amen.

CHAPTER 7

LENT AND FAMILY VALUES

First Sunday in Lent.

Recently we became aware of a tragedy that fell upon a broken family, once knitted together in harmony and affection. Over the years, the stress of pursuing a long cherished ambition, proved the undoing of a relationship, pledged until severed by death. It may have been the pain of separation, or the overbearing weight of the long struggle, or years of accumulated emotional disturbance. But aware that the one goal, when united as man and wife, they fought to achieve—was not to be hers proved the onset of disaster for the woman. She went into the garage, closed the door, started the engine. She committed suicide by inhaling fumes of carbon monoxide. She succumbed to the emotional and mental defeat of believing her life was no longer worth continuing. But we refuse to believe that death was the only solution open to her, or the sole avenue of relief available to her.

Without the quality of life sustained by values inherently enduring, one's prospects for happiness are greatly diminished. The season of lent is a good time to think about these things. For the good of our religious life, we ought to be in harmony with the Spirit of our Lord. It is good for us to refresh our memory about those things, which occurred so long ago, for our reconciliation to God—and to each other. But how does the concept of values, ideals of worth, or basic human fortitude become meaningful for us, known to us, and helpful?

The Promise.

This is the first Sunday in Lent, and in the yearly cycle of the seasons, it is the time when the days begin to lengthen. It is also the time in the church year, when we review the sacrifice of our Lord on the cross, where his body was broken and his blood shed for many, for the remission of sins.

When Jesus ascended, he left his confused and bewildered disciples behind to carry on his mission. But the disciples did not have all the gifts needed to stand up to a world bent on self-destruction. The disciples knew that our Lord's personal leadership was no longer with them. Yet Christ had said that it was to their advantage that he go. And he told them to wait for the promise of the Father; "For truly John baptized with water; but you shall be baptized with the Holy Ghost" (Acts 1:4-5).

All of God's promises carry with them blessings and gifts of spiritual significance. The promise spoken of by Jesus, soon to be realized, came in the gift of the Holy Spirit. In the Old Testament, the Spirit of God came mostly as an outward manifestation, when men sensed the presence and power of God. They were enlightened by it, moved by it, and endowed for a specific purpose; but they did not receive it as a permanent inner presence. The specific purpose may have been to build, to reign, or to prophesy. The craftsmen employed in the building of the Temple were filled with the Spirit; the seventy elders at Sinai prophesied under its influence; and it came upon David, when anointed to reign.

To the prophets, the promise of the permanent presence of the Spirit, shone as a light of hope through the long centuries of darkness. The significance lay in that the inner life was awakened, and an awareness of spiritual things came with the indwelling presence. Inwardly, the attendant new life principle affects the thinking, motivating, and feeling faculties of men. And it does so as a divine animating force, distinct from flesh and blood. The Spirit of the living God brings an enhancement to life with its presence, and it affects family values.

The Holy Spirit and Family Values.

Currently, we hear a great deal about family values. Yet the phrase is rather an indefinite concept. We need specific elements of worth, which we can attach to its meaning. Do we not mean the integrity of the family unit; the marriage community of man and wife and the children born to that union? Within the family, love, loyalty, and mutual affection ought to be every day manifestations. As a body of Christians, we hold to the concept that the family, instituted by God is the basic unit of society; that marriage is an honorable estate instituted by God, to be entered into reverently, discretely, and in fear of God.

For those who believe these things, the simple instructions of St. Paul still have validity for us—men ought to love their wives as Christ loved the church, and gave himself for it; and the wife ought to honor and reverence her husband. We can go through hardships, disappointments, and even suffering, because our religious convictions have the essential qualities that give endurance and fortitude to our existence.

In following the progress of the Lord Jesus during the weeks of the lenten season, we become aware that the integrity of the family involves kindness, consideration, and even sacrifice. At bottom, the question of family values involves our religious life. The convictions of this inner reality, is what we seek to strengthen during the weeks of lent. And in seeking our way, we can always look to the impulse and the soft leading of the Holy Spirit. The presence of the Holy Spirit with us, we believe, is the essence of our inner life.

The Reality of The Presence.

We, like the disciples of our Lord, know that the personal, physical presence of our Lord is no longer in the world as the Master of Galilee. But one of the wonders of our faith—in fulfilling his mission on earth and ascending to the Father—the Lord Jesus sent the Holy

Spirit to be with his people. And the Spirit came as a permanent, indwelling presence. He is one who stands alongside to help and sustain us, when we pass through the turbulent waters of suffering and loss. It is the Holy Spirit who leads us to the cross, who convicts the conscience of right and wrong, and who deepens the nature of our religious convictions.

With the Spirit's presence and comfort, no disappointment should affect us so severely, that relief is sought in oblivion. The idea of family values has significance in relation to our religious convictions as it can have in no other way. And it is in looking to the impulse of inner realities that affirms this for each of us individually. In lent we seek to draw closer to the Spirit of the Lord Jesus, to his spirit of kindness and consideration. We do so because we continually need reconciliation to God, family, and friends. We seek unity with our Lord. We look for appreciation and acceptance of his cross. We look to bring into our lives those qualities of our Savior's grace that give harmony and character to our days on earth.

In prayer and fasting, we seek to prepare ourselves to receive the saving way of God's forgiveness. We acknowledge our need of our Savior, the Lord Jesus Christ. We look to him to bring us through the shadows of the lenten season, and into the glory and light of his presence. We look to him who came to us out of the vast expanse of the heavens, when the world was encased in darkness. We look to him who brought us the knowledge of God's presence. And we affirm our conviction in things unseen, and in the surpassing grace of our Lord Jesus Christ.

CHAPTER 8

FAITH IN THINGS UNSEEN

Second Sunday in Lent.

As we embark on our lenten pilgrimage, we will walk with our Lord as he made his way through the appeals of the people. We note the watchful eyes of the temple scribes upon him. And we sense the gathering storm of the forces of opposition. From the Mount of transfiguration—where Christ was glorified before his disciples and acknowledged as the Son of God—the Lord Jesus descended again to be among those he came to serve. Christ knew that ultimately he would be rejected by the nation. And to this burden was added the weight of his approaching death on the cross. Still, the prospect of suffering and death never discouraged or deterred the Lord Jesus from completing his work of reconciliation.

We do Not Lose Heart.

The whole world is indebted to Louise Pasteur who founded the science of microbiology. In his discoveries, he worked out the prevention and cure for the disease of anthrax, for rabies, and cholera. He unveiled the cause of fermentation and the preservation of perishable foods. He gave the world the process of Pasteurization and founded the science of immunization. But the greatest wonder of all was the man, his character—and his belief in the advantageous outcome of his work. Why so? Because he accomplished all these things in the face of opposition. He drew opposition from enemies in the Academy of Science, from the public, and even from friends who refused to believe he would succeed. Although his wonders of discovery demanded hundreds of hours of hard labor, he never surrendered to the prophets of doom and ridicule. Pasteur refused to listen to the disdain of unbelievers; and he never ceased what he was certain was a noble endeavor. And Louis Pasteur never lost heart.

How like the Lord Jesus, Pasteur appeared in these facets of his character.

For the Lord Jesus, all through the first lenten season, the shadow of Good Friday drew ever nearer. Many of those who formerly followed him had turned away. The disciples misunderstood much of his teaching. And Christ faced fierce opposition from the religious authorities—who had already determined on his death, and the means by which it would be executed. Yet, never once did Christ falter, or turn back. Nor did he become discouraged.

The apostle Paul, having detailed some of the hardships he endured while engaged in labor for the Gospel, pointed to the establishment and growth of the Church. He wrote.

> So we do not lose heart... For this slight momentary affliction is preparing for us an eternal weight of glory beyond all comparison, because we look not to the things that are seen but to the things that are unseen; for the things that are seen are transient, but the things that are unseen are eternal.
> (2 Corinthians 2:16 RSV)

Though we may be limited in our efforts, subject to disease and suffer illness, we need not become discouraged. The experiences of life, some of which are painful, all enhance our maturity, our understanding, and our adaptability. Generally, most of our afflictions will pass. The apostle drew our attention to the things that are unseen: to our religious beliefs, to the spiritual inclination of the heart, and to the life of the soul. He stressed the transitory nature of things material—and laid emphasis on the eternal significance of things not seen. When we turn our thoughts on these things, we acknowledge that our religious convictions helped us get through times of bitterness—even when the weight of loss may have been overbearing.

When the Weight of Grief is Overbearing.

Some time back, we read in the newspaper, and it was broadcast nationally, about a newly born baby girl abducted from a maternity ward. It occurred a few weeks before Ash Wednesday. The drama could have ended in tragedy, but the authorities used tracker dogs and a helicopter, and located the abductors. The police found and returned the baby to her parents. In all, it had taken but a few days to recover the child. While the child was gone, the mother could only hope and pray for the baby's safe return. And she never lost the expectation, the earnest hope, that the baby girl would be returned. And how much more did the parents appreciate and love the infant daughter, now that they had her back unharmed and safe. Still, the possibility of loss had been very real, and had moved them deeply.

Occasions fall on us, when the loss and attendant grief can be overbearing. This is especially true, when related to a lost loved one. It is hard to measure the extent of loss. At times, it is difficult to acknowledge the reality of the loss, and to accept its actual occurrence. Grief lingers long and heavy on the heart. At other times, the memory of a loved one who has gone brings uncontrollable tears to our eyes. Perhaps, the tears come like the purging of the soul. We come to the realization that the one taken by death shall not return to us—like the baby girl abducted from the maternity ward. True, there is finality about death, but the end is not yet.

The second sibling born to my parents was named Salvador. He died when he was but two years old from an intestinal disorder. He was dearly beloved of my mother, because he was always attendant on her, expressing his affection, though he was only an infant. It seemed, she said, as though the tears would never stop. Salvador died six years before I was born. And I was twelve, when my mother told me this. It was eighteen years since our first Salvador's death, and tears still came to my mother's eyes.

"Why are you crying, Angelo?" she asked. I responded simply, "Because you are crying mother." She dried her eyes, gave me a hug, patted my rear, and sent me out to play. Then she got about preparing dinner. Later, much later, I asked how she got over it. "Not quite," she said. She was reading to me from her Bible: "but I had my religion." She had looked to the comfort of God, to her belief in the "hereafter," and to her unswerving faith in Christ our Lord.

In Christianity, we are endowed with a practical and helpful expression of religious beliefs. In our pilgrimage through the days of lent, we seek an awareness of these things; and an awareness of our Lord, on whom our trust is centered. We want to have the memory of our religious experiences refreshed—that even in the most pressing circumstances, when sorrow may fall upon sorrow—that we be neither discouraged, nor lose heart. We believe this is an acceptable goal in the lenten season.

When Death May Come.

There come those occasions, though few and far between, when all may be lost, even life itself. We may have planned carefully, worked diligently, and made ample provisions. And yet, due to things entirely out of our control, find that death will have overtaken us unexpectedly. But for Christians, the end is not yet.

> For we know that if this earthly tent we live in is destroyed, we have a building from God, a house not made with hands, eternal in the heavens. (2 Cor 5:1 RSV)

On January 18, 1912, Captain Robert Scott, leader of the National Antarctic Expedition, with four companions reached the South Pole. But it was only to discover that Roald Amudsen, the Norwegian explorer, had reached the South Pole first, more than a month before. The Norwegian explorer had good weather during his journey. And he left his tent in place to mark the location. Scott, of course, was deeply disappointed not to have reached the Pole first. But though disappointed, he could not afford to become discouraged. They had a return journey to their base camp of seven hundred miles. Of a sudden, the weather turned unfavorable, and their return trip became long, slow, and extremely difficult.

For weeks, the temperature dropped to 40 degrees below zero, and food ran low. Scott's party suffered from fatigue and weakness brought on by the exertion of their return trip. Every member sustained frostbite, and for days they were unable to move. Oates, a member of the polar party, knew he was too weak, holding the others back because of his condition. He went out into the cold of night, telling the others he would be gone for some time. But he never came back. The others had to continue their arduous journey without him. The weather permitting, as long as their strength endured they continued their struggle, barely able to move. But eventually, their strength played out and they were cut down by death. Eight months later, a search party found them, only eleven miles from their base camp. Scott and his men are remembered, because as long as they had breath, they refused to give in to the mean elements of the Antarctic Icecap.

What is the ultimate loss we can sustain? Is it not death itself? We will encounter opposition to some of our plans and ideas. We will experience hardship and loss. But in retaining belief in ourselves, and in the value of our objectives, we retain the possibility of success. We know that eventually the end comes to all. Look, said St. Paul, even though we should suffer death, and this earthly tent be destroyed, we have a building of God, a house not made with hands—eternal in the heaven. He was reminding his readers of the resurrection of the body and life everlasting.

Far into the return journey to base camp, Scott knew the end was near. In his last notes, he commended the care of his loved ones to the people of England; and himself and companions to the providence of God. We can attribute their courage and endurance to their religious convictions. In the lenten season, more than at any other time of the Church year, we unite in worship in the presence of the cross. It is the symbol of our religion, of service, and of sacrifice. In our hymns and in our prayers, we affirm our faith in things unseen. And we commend ourselves, our loved ones, and Christians everywhere to the providence of God.

CHAPTER 9

THE HEALING WATERS OF LENT

Third Sunday in Lent.

Lent is a season of refreshment, of grace, and of the renewal of our commitment to the way of the Lord Jesus Christ. The gentle sense of healing that comes with these days is a sign of forgiveness, absolution, and of the benevolence of God's love inherent in the season. To heal means to make well, to restore to soundness, and to cure the illness that may affect the body or soul. There is a brief passage in the book of Exodus which reads: "I am the Lord God that healeth thee" (Exodus 15:26).

Before a patient receives attention directed toward a cure, a diagnosis is made of the symptoms to determine the nature of the illness. There is an instrument called The Advanced Communications Satellite. Through this space satellite, people in rural areas can receive adequate medical care. A doctor miles away from the patient, can listen to his heart and review images, and serve for consultation. The specialists can aid in discovering the nature of the illness, give advice on its cured, and aid in recovery.

The Lenten season is a time to ask ourselves, how is our relationship with our heavenly Father, with each other, and how is our religious life progressing? What is the result of the diagnosis? Not as well as we would like, we can imagine.

Who can deny that we need a time of refreshment, our devotion made stronger, and our hearts given assurance in the reality of our religious convictions? The special worship services of the lenten season, the Scripture readings, the days of prayer and fasting are for our remedial benefit. These services are meant to draw us nearer heavenly things, to give an opportunity to the urging of our souls in seeking a closer affinity with him who opened the eyes of the blind and made the lame to leap as an hart. And the means that lead to our inner healing are neither painful nor difficult.

What are the Symptoms?

Prior to the recognition of Pediatric Surgery as a specialty by the American Medical Association, babies and little children died undergoing surgical procedures. What was wrong? Did anyone care or give the matter much consideration? Was it true that children were unable to undergo surgery? Anesthetized, many infants failed to recover from the induced sleep. Failure to recognize the problem, and to admit it could be corrected, did not help the situation. The children needed one who would fight for their cause, and struggle against entrenched reluctance to acknowledge the problem.

Several white knights emerged; among them was Everett Koop, former surgeon general of the United States. Early in his career, he served as surgeon at Children's Hospital in Philadelphia. He become a leading healer of babies and little children. All through his career, he struggled for recognition of pediatric surgery as a specialty. Through his work, and others like him, physical deficiencies once thought irremediable in little children, were repaired.

Doctor Koop conceived these little ones as children of God and of more value than many sparrows; and his means were simple and direct. He urged that they should be attended with surgical procedures uniquely fitted to their special needs—and fitted to their physiological make up. Suffering from physical deficiencies, infants and little children were not to be looked upon as distorted blotches of skin, bones, and tissue—but were to receive the best medical care possible. And in spite of obstacles imposed by limited and stunted mentalities, he succeeded. Doctor Everett Koop succeeded because he ran with good companions.

How so? Dr. Koop had to face the indifference of the "establishment" in the surgical field. Louis Pasteur was opposed by enemies in the Academy of Science; and the death of our Lord Jesus Christ was plotted by an entrenched and offended priesthood—that neither cared nor showed interest in those whom they conceived as the base things of the world. One interest group or another, not always moved by the purest motives, seems to erect a wall of opposition against the struggle to improve the well-being of the human race. It is apparent that were it not for those individuals courageous enough to do what they knew to be beneficial for humanity, we might still have slavery, sweat shops where children were compelled to labor long hours and expired early. And infectious disease would still be slaughtering people by the millions. Fortunately, God gave his servants grace to override all opposition.

The Healing Waters of Lent.

Although the Lord Jesus moved through the days of lent characterized as a man of sorrows, he remained sympathetic to the appeal of the people, attentive to their needs, and responsive to their request. We realize that time separates us from that ancient civilization in which the religious leaders questioned our Lord's authority to heal, and the means by which he achieved his results. Yet, our Lord came endowed with a power that was strange to them; and he was anointed with a Spirit they no longer possessed or believed in. Nevertheless, it is our Savior's presence that gives meaning and significance to the period of lent. And his presence comes with grace and truth.

The grace of our Lord Jesus Christ is kindness in excess of what may be expected. It is forbearance with our human nature, and compassion; and it is his disposition to be forgiving. A fault that seems almost inherent in human nature is the inability to deal with forgiveness. We need to be reminded of this, because we have an entire world out there that is in need of forgiveness. People go to doctors, counselors, and take medication to ease the pain of stress and anxiety. Yet, all along they hold deep personal hurts within, and remain at enmity toward each other. Some individuals suffer deeply, because they are unable to forgive themselves; and fortunately, the Lord God who heals the ills of the soul and mind, is also a God who searches the heart. The prophet Isaiah brought a message of consolation and about the heavenly Father's care, to an ancient people who lingered in a distraught condition of mind and soul.

> I have blotted out thy transgressions as a mist, and thy sins as clouds: return to me; for I have redeemed thee. (Isaiah 44:22)

The fault as seen by the prophet who spoke for God was that transgressions weighed heavily on the heart, and suppressed the life of the soul. And we may classify transgressions as anything which disturbed the people's relationship with God, and with each other. What had occurred? God interposed his benevolence at the very time when Israel had convinced themselves that God no longer cared, or had forgotten the nation he called and sanctified at Sinai: he blotted out their transgressions.

Isaiah drew their attention to the ease and rapidity with which their transgressions were expunged—and the remedial work begun. Whatever it was that had a detrimental effect on their relationship, whether with ancient Israel or with us today, God clears away like the wind sweeps away a mist. Return to me, said the Lord; for I have redeemed thee. Forgiveness and redemption were not offered on any condition precedent. The nation did not have to struggle or sacrifice to achieve these things; it needed only to receive and acknowledge their heavenly Father. What applied to the nation also applied to the individual. If God can forgive us for whatever the fault or transgression, it means that he accepts us just as we are. And it means further, that we can learn to forgive ourselves. One needs only to receive and turn to the Lord God. This is the time of grace, of refreshment, and of healing for all the ills that may affect the hearts and souls of the people. To the entire world out there that is in need of forgiveness the waters of lent will for ever continue to flow.

CHAPTER 10

THEY HAD BEEN WITH JESUS

Fourth Sunday in Lent.

After forty years of separation and loneliness, Moses was wandering in the Wilderness of Midian, tending the flocks of his father-in-law, Jethro, when he came upon the burning bush. The angel of the Lord, as a flame of fire was in the middle of the bush. And the bush was burning, yet not consumed. Moses said, I will turn aside and see this great sight, why the bush is not being consumed. That was the moment for Moses; for when the Lord God saw that he turned aside to see, he called to him out of the flames. And Moses became the servant of God from that moment on. Had he not paused to give this strange occurrence consideration, the world never would have heard about Moses. In the lenten season, we turn aside for periods of devotion, meditation, and spiritual renewal.

When Peter and John healed a lame man at the Gate Beautiful, the religious authorities asked them: "By what power or by what name did you do this?"(Acts 4:7). Peter replied.

> Be it known to you, that by the name of Jesus Christ of Nazareth, whom you crucified, whom God raised from the dead, by him is this man standing before you well. (Acts 4:8)

When the religious authorities saw the boldness of Peter and John, and were aware that they were uneducated men, they wondered: "For they acknowledged that they had been with Jesus."

Turning Aside.

During a lenten evening fellowship, an individual asked, "What are we doing here any way?" It was a good question. Why do we do the things we do as Easter Sunday draws near? We attend prayer fellowships, candle-light worship services, take holy communion on Maundy Thursday commemorating our Lord's last supper with his disciples, and attend worship services on Good Friday. Though it may not always be explicit in our minds, we seek to be near our Lord. We sense a heart yearning that cries out for the presence of the living God. We seek times of fellowship in his name, for meditation on his word, and to sense that we have been in his presence. For some of us, it may have been a long time since we felt a deep need of the soul and sought to fulfill it.

When Moses came upon that strange sight, it was not enough merely to stand off and look. He had to cease tending the flocks, draw near, and take a closer look. Like him, we must leave what we are doing for a few moments, and move near to be with the Lord. The result can be rewarding, new understanding, grace, and strength for the needs of the year ahead.

God Responds.

This movement on our part has always been the occasion. When God sees that we are attentive to things spiritual, he responds. There were others. Elijah, alone and despondent fled into the wilderness. When he came to the cleft in the rock, he stopped his flight, and waited for the Lord to appear. It was in the stilling of the elements that Elijah knew that the Lord approached. The silence came upon him like the echo of a brooding spirit. More often than not, the Spirit comes in the stillness, in the quiet moments of meditation, or during a simple, soul-felt prayer. The man at the lenten dinner asked, "What are we doing here?" God asked his servant, "What doest thou here, Elijah?"

So many things ran counter to his expectation. God's altars had been torn down, the people turned away, and his prophets slain with the sword. The sanctuary was empty. The long years of his seemingly hopeless task left the prophet spent, and his spirit nearly extinguished. Though he may not have voiced it, Elijah came for reassurance and renewal. God replied with love, his presence, and the power of his Spirit. The prophet was then enabled to complete his mission.

The years have exacted their toll on us also, and the harsh realities of a clashing world may run counter to the teachings of our ancient faith. It seems as though the altars have been torn down and the prophets ineffective. Many of the sanctuaries are half empty, and the fire on the golden altar is scarcely burning. "What doest thou here, Elijah?" We seek like Elijah of old for the help of the Lord to reach out to us. We look for God's presence and assurance to reach us through the confusion and contradiction of a society undergoing revolution. We want an answer, a solution to our most pressing questions about life and death. We turn to worship because our souls need communion with the Father of our spirits, and we look for his response. We need his power, grace, and light. We believe that God will answer in a time when he may be heard; so like Moses and Elijah, we have come to seek the Lord.

They Had Been With Jesus.

When Peter and John witnessed to the people, the people were amazed; and the religious authorities were compelled to acknowledge that these men had been with Jesus. During his earthly ministry, there were times when our Lord went away from the constant clamor of the crowd and demand on his person. He would go to be alone with his close disciples, Peter, James, and John. Together with these three, Jesus would go out on the lake or to a secluded place on the hillside, or to an upper room.

Once, they ascended Mount Hermon for prayer and meditation, and to be alone with God. While their Lord was deep in prayer, the disciples fell asleep. But the sleeping disciples were awakened by the sheer splendor of that occurrence. The cloud of God's presence covered the mountain top, and the glory of the Spirit shown through our Lord's apparel as he knelt in worship. The three disciples saw and heard it all. To Peter, James, and John came new understanding and the affirmation of their belief in Christ as the Son of God. They received knowledge and strength for the mission which lay ahead. Ever after, they would recall those moments, when they had ascended that holy mount with their Lord—and had seen his glory. The early church acknowledged their authority and leadership, because the early church knew that the disciples had been with Jesus.

There are times in the history of the church, when her mission may seem ineffective and unfruitful. It may seem that the darkness is gathering overhead. Peter came across such a period in the movement of the early church. Persecution had scattered the people and many were driven to the far corners of the empire. The constant struggle just to survive exhausted human resources, and there were those that gave up the cause of Christ. For a time, the church seemingly was without life. Peter wrote to remind them of God's power, grace, and glory. He wrote, telling them of the time when he, James, and John were with their Lord on that holy mountain.

> For we have not followed cunningly devised fables, when we made known unto you the power and coming of our Lord Jesus Christ, but were eyewitnesses of his majesty. For he received from God the Father honor and glory, when there came such a voice to him from the excellent glory, This is my beloved Son, in whom I am well pleased. And this voice which came from heaven, we heard, when we were with him on that holy mount. (2 Peter 1:16-18)

In the struggle with sorrow, frustration, and pain; when we feel overwhelmed and ineffective, we would do well to remember our Lord's power, grace, and glory. We will remember when he touched our souls with his grace, and our hearts were strangely moved. We will remember that when we came to be with our Savior, we sensed the gentle presence of the Spirit. We were empowered and renewed. How long are we to remember? We will remember as long, and as often as we need to. We will remember the time, the day, the very hour when during this lenten season we turned aside to be with the Lord Jesus.

CHAPTER 11

ON A DESERT ROAD

Passion Sunday.

There is a story about Philip, the Evangelist, narrated in the eighth chapter of the book of Acts. The incident took place on a desert road.

> And an angel of the Lord said to Philip, Rise and go toward the south to the road that goes down from Jerusalem to Gaza. And he rose and went. And behold, an Ethiopian, an eunuch, a minister of Candace, Queen of the Ethiopians, in charge of all her treasures, had come to Jerusalem to worship and was returning; seated in his Chariot, he was reading the prophet Isaiah. And the Spirit said to Philip, Go up and join this Chariot. So Philip ran to him, and heard him reading Isaiah the prophet, and asked: Do you understand what you are reading? And he said, How can I, unless some one guide me?
>
> And he invited Philip to come up and sit with him. Now the passage of scripture that he was reading was this.
>
> As a sheep led to the slaughter or a lamb before its shearers is dumb, so he opened not his mouth. In his humiliation justice was denied him.

Who can describe his generation? For his life is taken up from the earth. (Acts 8:26-33RSV)

About whom, asked the eunuch, does the prophet speak: about himself or about someone else. "And Philip began from this scripture and preached Jesus"
(Acts 8:38).

In Oberammergua, Baravia, every ten years, the Passion Play is given, portraying the suffering of the Lord Jesus Christ during his passion. As lent moves toward the closing weeks, through Good Friday, Holy Saturday, and Easter, we come to Passion Sunday. On this Sunday the Church reflects on the agony and suffering of Jesus. The time of Passion begins from the period following The Last Supper. The eunuch was reading from the Golden Passional. A Passional is a book describing the suffering of saints and martyrs. The Golden Passional is the fifty third chapter of the book of the prophet Isaiah, where the prophet, in a vision foretold the sufferings of Christ. It was this chapter that had gained the eunuch's attention.

On a Desert Road.

Philip, the evangelist, preached the fulfillment of prophecy. He was led by the Spirit away from the crowds, the cities, and the market place. He was brought far from the academies, seminaries, and places of intellectual attainment. On the desert road, Philip was far removed from the city's culture and the preoccupation with refinement. The evangelist was guided out into the solitude where nothing existed but heaven and earth, man and God, and the silence of the vast open spaces. Out here there was nothing to distract the thought process; and man must face God, life, death, sin, salvation, and eternity, and must face them all now.

A desert is a wilderness, an uncultivated region and without inhabitants; a dry and barren place. It was in the Wilderness of Midian that Moses learned obedience and trust in the God of his fathers. It was there that the angel of God's presence appeared to him, as a flame, in the middle of the burning bush. In the Wilderness of Paran the children of Israel learned faith and obedience through forty years of aimless wandering. And once again it was in an uninhabited place, on a desert road, that the fulfillment of the promise was revealed. For in many times past, and by different means, God spoke to the fathers about the sufferings of Christ.

Our Lord's Passion.

As the eunuch read the Passional, only one question troubled the Ethiopian: to whom did this passage apply, to the prophet Isaiah himself, or to some other person? Philip could well understand the eunuch's uncertainty, because for three years he had been with Jesus, and had misunderstood some of the Lord's teachings. When Jesus told them he would be delivered over to the Gentiles, mocked, scourged, abused and put to death, they remained uncomprehending and confused. Luke wrote that the disciples understood none of these things. It was on another road, on the way to Emmaus, where the risen Lord drew near to two of his followers, and was compelled to say.

> O foolish ones and slow of heart to believe all that the prophets have written. Was it not necessary that Christ should suffer these things and enter into his glory? (Luke 24:26)

And beginning with Moses and all the prophets, Jesus interpreted to them, in all Scripture, the things concerning himself. Many of our Lord's early followers had difficulty in believing all that the prophets had written. But not so the Ethiopian. He believed the prophet, that according to the word of the Father, the Redeemer would suffer and die. His only question was: "was it to be the prophet Isaiah, or some one else?" Philip began from this passage of Scripture and preached Jesus. The evangelist, having gone through the experience of Pentecost, and having seen his risen Lord, was reaching for the Ethiopian's heart.

Philip told him about the promise of the coming Redeemer, of his suffering and death, and of the coming of the Holy Spirit. That wonder working, unseen power that had led Philip out onto that lonely caravan route, had also moved the heart of the Ethiopian eunuch. His soul awakened by the revelation of the prophecy, made him receptive to the word of the Lord. He believed the Gospel message, and when all was made clear, he stopped the chariot; for even by this desert road the Lord God had provided. Here, like the stream of God's grace, was water. What was to prevent his baptism? Together they went down into the water, and Philip baptized the Ethiopian in the name of the Lord.

His Passion has Meaning for Us.

Life may seem empty at times, like a desert road in the middle of a wilderness, void of all spiritual reality and power. Even though we are surrounded by countless numbers of people, we can still feel isolated and alone. Flesh and blood can endure only so much, until the heart appeals for grace, for God, and for renewal of the spirit. The remedial touch of our Savior's Passion can do some of its best work for the Kingdom out in a desert, in a wilderness of wandering. Like Christ Jesus, John the Baptist was led out and nourished in the wilderness, and there he grew in strength, and in knowledge of the coming Kingdom of heaven. There in the desert God met him, spoke to his soul, energizing his spirit with divine fortitude. He was made like a mighty wind that could rend the rocks in pieces. He called for repentance and laid the axe to the root of the tree. Out in the wilderness John the Baptist was formed into a strong man of the Kingdom; indeed, he was its morning star.

God in Jesus Christ will meet us, when we are out on some lonely forsaken place in life. He will be there, and the encounter will come as if face to face. Nothing else will really matter for the moment. Heaven and earth could pass away, and it would not really matter at all. When isolated or alone, when flesh and blood can endure no more, when the soul pleads for grace, Our Savior will be there to help in time of need.

Our Lord was led into the wilderness for forty days, where he struggled with truth and reality, where he fought for his church, its creation, and for its people. Christ mediated on the passage from Isaiah, where it spoke of the sheep led to the slaughter; and he thought on his coming agony, the crucifixion, and the cross. There he stood and fought, and vanquished the power of evil; and because of this he is worthy to receive honor, and power, and glory, and dominion for ever.

Thus, Christ became our way into the Kingdom of heaven and our peace with God. His Spirit can lead us from any place on a desert road to truth, light, and grace. In the quiet stillness of a desert night, or in the dawn of a new day, during the first rays of light from the east, we ought to look for the coming of the Spirit.

And if we expect it, and look for it, like the still small voice of the morning, the Spirit will speak the words: "See and know, on the Cross, the Lamb of God who takes away the sins of the world, gave his life to lead us back to the Father, to grace and glory; and in him, to life everlasting.

CHAPTER 12

IF THESE BE SILENT

Palm Sunday.

On the first Palm Sunday many centuries ago, the people became excited about their religion. They shouted, spread their garments on the road, and voiced their praise to God. They waved palm branches, crying out: "Blessed be the King that cometh in the name of the Lord: peace in heaven, and glory in the highest" (Luke 19:38). For one hour, perhaps for a whole day, caution was thrown to the wind, and the people rejoiced at the coming of the prophet of Nazareth. The people's religious fervor ran high as they greeted Jesus on his entry into the city of Jerusalem.

An Enthusiastic Acclaim.

In his last week before the crucifixion, Jesus of Nazareth descended the Mount of Olives, and came to the city of Jerusalem. It seemed as though he entered in triumph as the Son of God, the Lord, and king of Israel. The people appeared to have gone into frenzy. They got out of control, and there were those who feared things could have gotten out of hand. The priests became fearful, and addressed the Lord Jesus. They requested that he rebuke his disciples and the crowd, bidding them to be silent. Jesus replied: "If these be silent, the very stones would cry out" (Luke 19:40).

Yet, the people, and even the Lord's disciples, were in error, not about the Savior's person or his claims, but about the nature of his Kingdom. The people wanted a king who would drive out the Romans, and restore the land and kingdom to Israel. Their words of praise indicated that their monarchy would always be related to God. Their kingdom under David was a time of glory and expansion for Israel. They longed again for the days of grandeur, but the Romans occupied and ruled their land with an iron hand.

When the people shouted, praised God, and acclaimed Jesus as king, they frightened the priests and the authorities with their enthusiasm. There was the ever present danger of severe reprisal, if the crowd got too far out of control. The people would be charged with insurrection. Unable to silence the multitude, the authorities appealed to Jesus, but to no avail. The Kingdom had come. For, indeed, Jesus came in the name of the Most High, as the only begotten of the Father, and the Holy Spirit was all about him. Such was the effect and power of the moment. And our Lord knew beyond question that if all these people were silenced, the stones would cry out in acclaim. Christ was aware that death could not hold him, or silence contain the voice of the multitude. The wild, fervent, enthusiastic acclaim of Palm Sunday, continued, at least for a few glorious hours.

Have we ever been filled or even touched lightly, with religious fervor? Is there anything enthusiastic about the expression of our religious convictions? More often than not, we are the sane and quiet ones; and there is surely nothing wrong in this. And while excitement really never bothered the people, it always troubled the priests. They were unable to cope with it. And I imagine that today, if we got a little out of hand with religious fervor, some individual would bid the Master rebuke us. In spite of all that, on one day long ago, Jesus of Nazareth was greeted with an enthusiastic acclaim as he entered the city of Jerusalem. But it was a city that he characterized as not knowing the things that made for peace, or the day of its visitation.

Their Ardor Faded Away.

When Moses ascended the mount to be with God, and then came down to address the people, he had to put a veil over his face, because the splendor of God's presence was too strong about him for the people to look on his face. Slowly, the glory of God's presence receded, and Moses could come into the presence of the people without the veil. The excitement of our Lord's coming in the name of the Father also faded away, and the shouts of praise gave way to silence. Like a shooting star flashing across the heavens, the Savior's coming to Jerusalem lit up the hopes of the people; and just as quickly, the momentary acclaim diminished. What happened?

It was simply that acclamation alone was not enough to make the hope of God's promise endure. There must be more than an intense interest in religious matters. The giving of their garments could no more hold the people to the cause, than the palm fronds could hold the glory of the occasion; for by the end of the day the palm fronds were scattered to the winds. The Savior was aware of their mis-directed objectives, and looking over the city, he wept for it: "Would that it might know the things that made for peace."

Not only did the splendor of his coming to Jerusalem diminish, his followers were also beginning to drop off. Since Jesus was not going to restore the kingdom to Israel, disappointment turned to despair; and by Good Friday, despair was expressed in the rejection of Jesus of Nazareth. The Savior's Kingdom was not of this world. The Kingdom of heaven came with a grace that healed, forgave, and redeemed the soul from destruction. Its essence was spiritual, in a fellowship with the Lord Jesus and the Father.

But the crowd as a whole was not in tune with the deep inner realities of the spirit. Nor was there a sincere commitment to the Christ who came in the name of the Most High; and yet, without sincere commitment to Christ as Savior, there was nothing. In the expression and experience of the Christian religion, our relationship to the Savior is one of faith unfeigned, springing from a sincere heart. On the first Palm Sunday, the multitude's enthusiasm and the shedding of their garments were of no lasting value. They lack the essential elements of faith and worship of which their acts ought to have been the tokens. There was no heart-turning to the Lord God. The one thing which the Savior most desired, they refused to give. And they turned away from Jesus as the promised Redeemer of Israel. Christ wept for the city that so greatly misunderstood the nature of God's dealing with men. And as night drew near, the wonder of the day entirely dissipated.

Rejected of Men.

We would do well to be attentive to the events of the first Holy Week. The acclaim that was raised on Palm Sunday was gone, followed not only by our Savior's rejection, but by demands for his death. The events moved swiftly. There was the cleansing of the Temple, where Jesus had driven out the money changers. This was followed by The Last Supper with his disciples, where our Lord instituted the sacrament of Holy Communion. But already betrayal was at work in the heart of Judas, as he quickly left the upper room. After the sacramental meal, the Lord Jesus retired to the Garden. And while he prayed, the mob of the chief priest came to arrest him, as he was betrayed by a kiss. As they took our Lord away, the disciples followed far behind. Before Pilate, the rejection came to a head, and Peter later told what had occurred.

> But you denied and rejected the holy and righteous one, and asked for a murderer to be released to you. (Acts 3:14)

The crowd again cried out in acclamation, when Jesus was brought before Pilate and the Roman tribunal. But their voices were raised in favor of Barabbas. Jesus was rejected, and Pilate marveled that he remained silent. The Roman governor could find no fault in him, and he suspected the motives of those who had delivered him up. What was to be done with Jesus? Away with such a one, the multitude cries, encouraged by the temple agents. Away with the king of the Jews asked Pilate, still trying to release the Lord Jesus? Away with him, cried the mob again, "We have no king but Caesar;" and that sealed our Savior's fate. It was apparent to Pilate that Jesus was to suffer and die according to that which was written by the prophets— even though he had done no wrong. Within the providence of God, the events of holy week followed their appointed course. From the triumphant entry into the city of Jerusalem, to the betrayal of Judas and the final rejection before Pilate were but a few days.

As this Lenten season nears the cross, religious sentiment may run high among the people of our Savior's church. And it is a thing highly to be desired. We trust that it will be more than a fleeting expression of religious fervor. Lent is a time of heart-turning to the Lord Jesus. Though our voices may be hushed in worship, our souls ought not to be unmoved. Attentive to the religious significance of the lenten season, we look for a clear perspective of our religious convictions. We seek a closer affinity with the Christ of God. We remember the words of St. Paul written to Titus: words never understood by those who rejected the Savior of men.

> According to his mercy he saved us, by the washing of regeneration, and renewing of the Holy Ghost: Which he shed on us abundantly through Jesus Christ our Savior; That being justified by his grace, we should be made heirs according to the hope of eternal life. (Titus 3:5-7)

CHAPTER 13

THIS IS MY BODY

Maundy Thursday Communion.

It was the time of the Passover, and the Lord Jesus expressed to his disciples the feelings that stirred in his soul: "I have earnestly desired to eat this Passover meal with you before I suffer" (Luke 22:15). He knew that the cross was before him. Within the festive season of the Passover, which commemorated Israel's deliverance form Egypt, there should have been peace, harmony, and gratitude among the people. Instead, there was fear and suspicion abroad. Plots and counter plots were being hatched, as the chief priests and scribes conspired how they might put to death the prophet of Nazareth.

Nor was the conflict limited to the sacred halls of the Temple. The struggle had assumed spiritual proportions, as powers and principalities contested the issue; and Satan entered Judas called Iscariot, who sold himself to betray his Master. Yet our Lord and his disciples would partake of the meal together. They gathered in a quiet place, removed from the eyes and ears of the Temple agents. It was an unobtrusive, obscure upper room, which two of the disciples had obtained for this purpose. It was to be Christ's last hour together with the men he had called to labor with him in the Kingdom of heaven.

As we share the elements of bread and wine, we commemorate our Lord's last Passover meal with his disciples, before he was subjected to the suffering of the cross. Maundy Thursday, the day before Good Friday was originally observed with the ancient rite of foot washing, as a sign of humility, meekness, and service. This task was performed by our Lord for his disciples after the meal at the Last Supper. Within the Protestant communion, the significance of the day was slowly transformed and celebrated in commemoration of our Lord's last supper with his disciples—where Christ instituted the sacrament of Holy Communion.

Holy Communion has about it the aura and drama of the incidents occurring in the upper room of long ago. Here, Jesus warned Simon Peter that Satan desired to sift him as wheat, where thoughts of betrayal churned in Iscariot's mind commingled with shame and guilt, and where the disciples troubled with self-doubt, asked one after another, "Is it I?" To calm their fears, steady their minds, and give them grace for renewal, amidst the elements of bread and wine, our Lord promised to pray for them, "that their faith not fail."

Christ enlightened the disciples on the mystical and spiritual meaning of Holy Communion, as he applied the bread and wine to himself and his mission.

Although the immediate impact of the Savior's words were lost on them that night, when Jesus had gone to be with the Father, the disciples were to recall, time and time again, that hour of high spiritual drama, when grace had been poured over their souls like living water. This sacrament, initiated on Maundy Thursday in that distant upper room, has retained its spiritual meaning and mystical appeal for all who have turned to the Lord Jesus as the Christ of God.

The Savior's Conception of The Last Supper.

> And the Lord Jesus took the bread, and when he had given thanks, he broke it and gave it to them saying.
>
> This is my body which is given for you. Do this in remembrance of me. And likewise the cup, after supper, saying, This cup which is poured out for you is the new covenant in my blood. (Luke 22:19-20)

The words of the Savior mirrored the thoughts of Christ's perception of his life, mission and its consummation. He gave this interpretation, knowing that in less than a day he was to suffer at the hands of sinful men. The mystery of the incarnation and the cross were revealed in the mystical and spiritual application of our Lord's body to the world's redemption. His body was given for the life of the world, and his blood was shed for many, for the remission of sins. He spoke about the new covenant, which came with a much better promise: it was given a spiritual endowment by the Father of lights. Jesus conceived his mission as ordained of God. It had as its objective the reconciliation of men and women, once estranged from God's love, bringing them to peace and nearness to the Father through the suffering of his cross.

The bread was broken and eaten as the meal progressed, but the dedication of the cup, containing the wine, came at the end of the supper, after the meal was completed. To the church, Holy Communion became an outward and visible sign of inward, spiritual grace; and Christ, the source of her spiritual life. In that ceremony, our Lord sustained the life of his disciples. He upheld their courage, endowed them with gifts and abilities necessary for their mission; and he bestowed upon them spiritual perception.

This was later confirmed by the coming of the Holy Spirit at Pentecost. How did Jesus do this? He did it by giving them his power, presence, and Spirit. As the disciples went about their Gospel mission, he came to stand by them, and to strengthen them when their way grew difficult. He restored their souls, when their spirits grew faint, and he was with them in their sorrows. No matter what the world might do to them, when they finished their course, their Lord would bestow on them a crown of righteousness and everlasting life.

The Savior's conception of the sacrament was related to his life and work. Through it, he explained that his life and mission were those of service, sacrifice, and reconciliation. And whether in the first century, or in our present century, service, sacrifice, and reconciliation are still the elements which make up the essential mission of the church. When the church is no longer willing to sacrifice for the fruitful outcome of its goals, it will have fallen short of its great commission.

The Impact of the Sacrament on the Disciples.

The effect and grace of that ceremony with their Lord were not immediately apparent on the disciples. They were not yet fully formed, or ready to begin their mission of reconciling the world to the bosom of the Father. They were unaware of the grace that had been given them, and did not know the power that would come upon them. And whether or not they confessed it, they were still fearful of the mob, mistrustful of the religious authorities, and doubtful of their own abilities. Nevertheless, all this was to change, and it did so dramatically.

After the events of holy week, and Pentecost, when the Spirit came upon them in power, and the understanding of their minds spiritually enhanced, they would remember. They would recall that fellowship of grace and spirit, when they had gathered in the presence of The Eternal and the bread of life was broken for them. Spirit to spirit had spoken, and their Lord had prayed for them. In truth, they remembered much more, recalling his teachings, Gospel, and their great commission. And they would remember the Lord Jesus in the breaking of the bread.

So meaningful had Holy Communion become to early Christianity that it evolved into the central act of the church in worship. In its celebration, the aura of the Savior's presence was about the entire sanctuary where they met. It flooded over their fellowship, and sensed in their souls. The sacrament brought them the ever present, living reality of their Lord's presence. The spiritual energy of the bread and wine, bringing the apostolic church the realization of the companionship of the Lord Jesus with all his redeeming power, enabled them to conquer an empire.

In the growth of the Kingdom of heaven, those endowed with the grace of our Lord Jesus Christ, took the Gospel to the far corners of their world.

The Meaning of Maundy Thursday Communion for Us.

This religious ceremony, instituted in that upper room of ancient times, has retained all its spiritual meaning and force. Its mystical appeal still pulls at our heartstrings, drawing us into the presence of our great God and Savior, the Lord Jesus Christ. We have united in worship on Maundy Thursday, because this is the day that commemorates the beginning of this sacrament and the promise of our Lord's presence and power. We also remember the promise of our Savior's mediatorial office, in the sanctuary not made with hands, that he pray for us that our faith fail us not. We come to this central act of the church in worship because it is in line with the simple command of our Evangel: "Do this in remembrance of me."

And when more appropriately, than on the day in which we remember the beginning of Holy Communion in the church of Jesus Christ.

We come to this sacrament as God's people have always come, because we wish to be included in the blessings of the Kingdom of heaven. We seek him whom our hearts desire, and long to feel the presence of the Spirit, quietly whispering to our souls, "I am thy salvation." In the presence of the elements of the sacrament, we sense our unity with that great cloud of unseen witnesses to the grace and glory of God, who make up the body of Christ and the church triumphant. We have come to have the bread of life broken to us, as it was in the beginning. And like the disciples of our Lord, we acknowledge our need of spiritual renewal, and to have our faith enhanced by our communion with the Son of God.

We accept that this sacrament is our Lord's body, that these creatures of bread and wine speak to us of higher things, and will lead us to life everlasting. As we worship in praise and gratitude, our petition is that he who walks on the wings of the wind, "Who makes his angels spirits, and his ministers a flame of fire" (Psalm 104:3-4), might touch us with his grace. That he be gracious to us and lay his hand on us, and fill us with his peace. We confess in the presence of the bread and wine, that our citizenship is in heaven, that we "look for a city that hath the foundations, whose builder and maker is God." Amen.

CHAPTER 14

HE WAS RECKONED WITH THE TRANSGRESSORS

Good Friday.

Good Friday is the Friday before Easter Sunday. On this day, when Pontius Pilate served as the procurator of Judea, the Lord Christ Jesus was brought before the Roman tribunal. He had been delivered over to prosecution by the leaders of his people. This was the final rejection of the one who should have redeemed Israel by the religious authorities of the nation. The Roman proconsul found no wrong in Jesus. And three times he sought to release him. But the chief priest, the scribes, and the mob inflamed by the temple agents, would not relent. Cries for the cross never ceased. And though neither Pilate nor Herod found anything in the prophet of Nazareth deserving death, the Christ of God was delivered over, that their demands should be granted. A jealous and offended priesthood had planned the demise of Christ and his religious movement.

The disposition of the judgment was crucifixion on a cross between two condemned criminals. In his final hours, the promised Redeemer come from the heart of God, *"was reckoned with the transgressors"* (Luke 22:37). But God who works wonders, penetrated the veil with his grace—and from the cross of Christ, the doors of the Kingdom of heaven were open wide. How did this come about? What had motivated the principal characters in the drama of the ages? And what significance have these events for us?

The Issues of Life Spring From the Heart.

For Judas Iscariot, one of our Lord's disciples, ambition frustrated and gone wrong, together with greed, led to betrayal. The chief priests, suspicious and filled with envy at Christ's success with the people, moved as the prime schemers of the plot. Their impulses, nurtured with unconcealed hatred, broke out into murder. And with the people, disappointed hopes, which conceived vengeance, prompted the mob to raise the cry for the cross time and time again. But Pontius Pilate, though a coward, was no fool. He knew beyond a reasonable doubt, that because of envy they had delivered up Jesus of Nazareth. Nor did he believe that the devotion of the multitude before the judgment seat of imperial power was so far elevated over that of the Romans, that they had no king but Caesar. Nevertheless, rather than to trouble himself with the proper exercise of his authority, he gave the Lord Jesus over to their will.

Throughout the history of the human race, the basic issues of life have remained the same. Weakness and moral irresolution always lead to lack of proper action. And the forces of evil and wrong win by default. When the right is more difficult to execute than the wrong, when it may cause inconvenience or pain, the tendency of human nature is to take the easy way out. Pontius Pilate is remembered today, not because he sidestepped a matter of the proper disposition of justice, but because he attempted to wash his hands of Jesus Christ. And every school boy and every school girl knows he failed.

The act of Judas Iscariot proclaimed to the entire world that he had sold himself for gain to do evil. His act also revealed that neither his heart nor his soul had been right with the Lord Jesus. To obtain the benefits of spiritual blessing, one cannot serve the Kingdom of heaven for personal gain; and a mission of service and self-sacrifice for others was that furthest removed from the mind of Judas Iscariot. Holding the purse and mean ambition, had distorted his perspective. Yet, throughout all the events that had brought the cross to pass—all the characters in the central drama of Good Friday were in tune with each other—both in their means and in their attempts of disclaimer.

Cunning, deception, and evil means can never be harmonized with God's way, or with our Lord's Kingdom of peace and righteousness. When shame and guilt grew overwhelming in his soul and conscience, Judas Iscariot sought to cleanse himself by returning the tainted pieces of silver. He knew he had betrayed innocent blood. But this self-cleansing and relief were denied him. The chief priests, like Pontius Pilate, refused to accept any blame for Iscariot's act of betrayal. Iscariot's conscience—and the state of his soul—were, they confessed, of no concern to them who were the spiritual leaders of the people. Still, they who exercised the mediatorial office of the throne of grace had entered into a criminal conspiracy with Judas to do that which was wrong. And they gave him money to seal the bargain.

Judas Iscariot betrayed the trust, which the Lord Jesus had placed in him. Pontius Pilate surrendered the honor and integrity of his judicial office. And the chief priests and scribes had plotted to commit murder and killed the prince of life. And—they concluded by neglecting their priestly duties, in that they denied atonement for sin to a soul headed toward perdition. And hence, they had profaned the nature of their high calling. And yet, they had reckoned the Lord's Christ as numbered with the transgressors.

How did the Lord Jesus view this? Jesus attributed the conduct of those who had condemned him to lack of spiritual affinity with, and knowledge of, God. They had never been endowed with God's Spirit, or had made a heart-surrender to God's will. Faith in God, even for the chief priests, is a matter of the heart, and involves the inclination of the soul. True faith has always looked to the saving way of God's forgiveness as a gift of his grace. But the Lovely Evangel of God's grace was a thing unknown to the religious authorities who rejected the Lord Jesus—and consigned him to the cross.

The Intent of the Religious Authorities.

The way of the world had worked its way on the Lord Jesus. And on the day we commemorate as Good Friday, he was nailed to the cross between two offscourings of humanity. As the leaders of the people gathered about the foot of the cross to see their desire executed, they ridiculed and mocked Christ as he suffered. And yet, God is not mocked with impunity. The multitude and the followers of Christ stood watching the incidents that took place about the cross. They saw the soldiers cast lots for the Savior's garments, and heard the rulers scoff at him while he hung on the cross:

> He saved others; let him save himself, if he is the Christ of God. (Luke 23:35)
> Let him come down now from the cross, and we will believe in him. (Matthew 27:42)

Although the religious authorities refused to believe in the Lord Jesus, as he hung on the cross, they asked for a sign of the Savior's messianic character. They wanted an exercise of his divine power to prove, in their presence, that he was the Son of God. Because of their impenitent hearts, their sign would be that of Jonah. And even if John the Baptist had come back from the grave, so steep were they in their own self-righteousness that they would not have believed. Their words were, in reality, a sign of their contempt for the man of sorrows. Their spirit was also expressed in one of the condemned thieves. Though he too hung on a cross, he took on the mental attitude of the mob.

The impenitent thief conceived his end as irredeemable. And having lost his soul, he had lost all: "Are you not the Christ? Save yourself and us" (Luke 23:39). What had he done? The impenitent thief hurled his last curse at the Lord God, and at his Christ. Having learned in sin, he embodied the spirit of the chief priests, his words echoing their disdain for the prophet of Nazareth. The cross came as the concluding act of the leaders' rejection of the Lord Jesus—as the end of their jealousy, envy, and hatred of him who was meek and lowly of heart.

Through the cross, the chief priests intended more than getting rid of one who had come as the Christ. The aim of the religious authorities—of having disposed of Jesus without the gates of the city, like an offering for sin—and the instrumentality of the cross—*was oblivion.* They had in mind the death of the Christian movement, of the memory of Christ, and of all hope that resided in the Lord Jesus as the Son of God. They wanted Jesus forgotten completely, absolutely, like one time out of mind. But they failed in their design.

Grace, Greater Than All Our Sins.

It is written, "God taketh the wise in their own craftiness" (1 Cor 3:19). There, at the cross, the plan of the religious authorities began to fall apart. While the impenitent thief possessed the spirit of the mockers, he was silenced by the other dying thief. Did he not fear even God? His ravings could only have been those of a man driven mad with pain. The penitent thief did not have the spirit or the attitude of those who mocked beneath the three crosses. As he hung on a cross like the Savior, in his own personal agony, he turned to the Lord Jesus. He acknowledged his own criminal trespass, and confessed that they suffered justly. And to the other dying thief, the impenitent one made know that Christ, who hung between them, had done no wrong. The penitent thief, in his confession, had looked to the saving way of God's forgiveness, and the Spirit of the Most High God had given him a revelation. He had confessed his sin to the dying Jesus. He understood that the Lord's Christ was crucified with them because he claimed to be the Son of God, Israel's promised Messiah.

The penitent's thief's spirit was other than that which moved the jeering multitude. It had been the Holy Spirit, coming through the veil, that touched his soul, and which made him receptive to the grace of God—so near by. Indeed, though only the dying, confessing thief was blessed with spiritual perception; nevertheless, about the cross, the presence of the living God was nearer than breathing, closer than hands and feet. Sensing this, the penitent's soul awakened, and his heart was touched by the finger of God. His response to the Lord Jesus emerged from a life that, for one brief hour, pulsated with a new beat: "Lord, remember me, when thou comest into thy kingdom" (Luke 23:42).

What had occurred between the penitent thief and the Lord Jesus? As the Savior hung on the cross in all his humiliation, the penitent acknowledged Christ as the promised Redeemer. He turned to the dying Christ in full confession as Savior and Lord. Yet, has it not ever been so with the Lord Jesus? He never turns away from any man or women, regardless of their former character, quality of life, or however imperfect their expression of faith. Though all may not have been spoken between them, our Lord understood the dying thief's petition clearly: it was a request for pardoning grace, absolution, for the blessing of God, and admission into the Kingdom of heaven. And our Lord responded:

Truly, I say to you, today you will be with me in paradise.
(Luke 23:43)

There, at the cross, on Good Friday so many years ago, God's grace penetrated the veil of darkness. God's grace frustrated the work of evil doers, and opened wide the doors of the Kingdom of heaven for all who would turn to the Lord Jesus. Even so, the Lord Jesus had not come to call the righteous, but to restore that which sin had blighted. He came to bring release to the captives, bind the wounds of the people; and having made atonement for sin, to lead us back to the Father. And in so coming, Christ extended his invitation to all who would enter the Kingdom of Heaven. Neither the cross, nor the grave, can withhold our Savior's grace. And our Savior's glory followed on his resurrection, whose glory shall be consummated in the New Heaven and New Earth—and it all began on the first day of the week.

CHAPTER 15

EASTER SUNDAY

ON THE FIRST DAY OF THE WEEK

The Story.

It was on the first day of the week, at the early dawn, that the women who had followed the Lord Jesus went to the tomb. And they found the stone rolled away, and they did not find the body. And two men stood by them in dazzling apparel, and said to them: "Why do you seek the living among the dead? Remember how he told you, that the Son of man must be delivered into the hands of sinful men, be crucified, and on the third day rise." And returning from the tomb, the women told all this to the disciples, but these words seemed to them as an idle tale, and they did not believe the women (Luke 24:1-12).

At the Early Dawn.

At the early dawn, before the breaking of the day, in the stillness of the morning, that is when the whole wide world is awakening. That is the time when amazing things, and even miracles, can occur. That was the time when Mary Magdalene, Joanna, and Mary, the mother of Jesus, went to the tomb. And what an amazing story they told the disciples. They went to see Jesus. They did not find the body. They had seen visions of angels, the angel of the resurrection, who said that Jesus was alive, that he was risen even as he had said, at the early dawn before the breaking of the day.

> This was also the early dawn of the New Testament faith: Concerning Jesus of Nazareth, who was a prophet mighty in deed and word before God and all the people whom the rulers crucified [but whom God raised up]. (Luke 24:19-20)

The good news that the Lord Jesus had risen was proclaimed first, not to the disciples, or even to the inner circle of Peter, James, and John, but to the women who had attended the Lord Jesus. The good news was revealed to the women who had cared for the Savior's needs, washed his feet, and had anointed him for his burial. It was to Mary Magdalene, to Joanna, and to Mary, the mother of Jesus, to whom the glad tidings were first given. And today, throughout the length and breadth of the land, at the early dawn, millions are gathered in the Savior's name in sunrise services to worship Jesus of Nazareth, Lord of the resurrection morning. They wait with hope and expectancy for the coming of this day, and the message of the three women to the disciples, and to all men: "He is not here, but he is risen," at the early dawn—before the breaking of the day.

The Stone was Rolled Away.

I would imagine that the first thing which struck the women as amazing was that the stone was rolled away. The stone had been placed there to seal the tomb, and was meant to close up the grave of Jesus. But the stone that the builders rejected had already become the chief corner stone of the Kingdom of Heaven. By the early dawn, the seal had already been opened. Quite clearly, all three women could see that the stone was rolled away. And we hear as a foreshadowing of a new day, the words from the Revelation of St. John.

> Worthy is the Lamb that was slain to receive power, and riches, and wisdom, and strength, and honor, and glory, and blessing.
> (Revelation 5:12)

Indeed, worthy is the lamb that was slain to open up the seals, and to declare unto men the counsels of God. The two Marys and Joanna were also worthy to open up the seals, and to declare to the disciples what had occurred, what great things God had done at the tomb, before the breaking of the new day. But like when they had fallen asleep in the Garden, the disciples were still slow of heart to believe all that the prophets had written. And like foolish ones, they thought the good news brought to them by the women were only idle tales.

But a few things still perplexed them: the body was gone, the stone was rolled away, and Jesus had said that on the third day he would rise. This was not only the first day of the week, but it was also the third day since the crucifixion. The disciples wondered about the story. On the first day of the week, at the early dawn, the stone had been rolled away—and their women had seen visions of angels

Why do You Seek the Living Among the Dead.

But note what the angel of the resurrection said to the two Marys and to Joanna: "Why seek you the living among the dead? He is not here, but is risen, even as he had said." You seek Christ, the crucified one: he is not here. He has risen. He is now the risen Savior. He is Christ whom God declared to be his Son by the power of the resurrection; and you will not find the living among the dead. And how true this is for us today. We do not base our faith on an empty tomb or upon an open grave, but on a risen and resurrected Lord. Our Savior is one whom death could not hold, who has opened up the seals, who rose victorious from the grave in the power of the Spirit of holiness, and ascended to glory at the right hand of God exalted: for it was necessary that Christ should suffer all these things, and then to enter into his glory.

For three days, the disciples were fearful and confused, perhaps, for more than three days. We had hoped, they said to each other. We had dreamed, we had believed that it should have been he that would have redeemed Israel. With the crucifixion of their Lord, those hopes had come to a near end. The news brought by the three women was unable to break through the darkness of their spiritual hearts, caused by the night of Holy Saturday. Only the three women remembered, when the angel of the resurrection spoke to them. They remembered all that had been written in the prophets; while the disciples still thought of the living as among the dead.

Our Savior had to draw near to them on the way to Emmaus, and make himself physically known to them before they believed. Our Lord did so on the third day.

> They returned to Jerusalem, and found the eleven gathered together, and them that were with them, saying, The Lord is risen indeed, and hath appeared to Simon. And they told what things were done in the way, and how he was known to them in the breaking of the bread. (Luke 24:33-35)

And as they were saying this, suddenly, Jesus himself stood among them. The disciples were startled, thinking they saw only a spirit. They still had difficulty in believing what was written in the Scriptures. Then slowly, gently, with grace and compassion, the Teacher come from God opened the eyes of their understanding. With love, patience, and grace; that is ever how one must deal with the slow of heart:

> Why are you troubled and why do questionings rise in your hearts? See my hands and my feet, that it is I myself; handle me and see; for a spirit has not flesh and bones as you see that I have. (Luke 24:38-40)

And the Lord Jesus opened the eyes of their understanding to comprehend the teachings of the Scriptures:

Thus it was written, that Christ should suffer and on the third day rise from the dead, and that repentance and forgiveness of sins should be preached in his name to all nations. (Luke 24: 46-47)

And when the disciples departed from their risen Lord, they returned to Jerusalem with great joy. Now, at last, they had joined the company of their women; and no more would they seek the living among the dead. Their hearts had burned within them, when the Lord had walked with them along the way, and their spirits quickened. This had been the third day, when our risen Lord had drawn near to two of his disciples on the way to Emmaus.

On The First Day of The Week.

On the first day of the week, at the early dawn, the stone had been rolled away; and Jesus Christ the Lord of glory had risen from the grave. On the first day of the week, the power of fear over death was broken, and Christ our Lord was declared to be the Son of God through the power and Spirit of the resurrection. At the early dawn, before the breaking of the day, on the first day of the week, Christ had changed the sunset of Good Friday into the sunrise of Easter morning. Lord! What a morning, what a morning indeed!

The Savior's resurrection changed the entire concept of the cross; and its concept was changed "by reason of the glory that excelleth." Now, since the first day of the week, the cross is the symbol of the Christian faith, of hope, of redemption, and of life everlasting. Christ is our way of access to God; because every one who truly comes to the Lord Jesus comes to him as the Christ of the cross. Moreover, on the first day of the week, the Holy Spirit manifested abroad the reality of an endless life for all who embrace the risen Christ as Savior and Lord. It was at the early dawn, on the first day of the week, when the stone was rolled away; when the angel spoke to the women, and they remembered all that was written by the prophets concerning Jesus of Nazareth.

On the first day of the week, ever since that grand resurrection morning, the faithful in Christ Jesus have gathered to worship in his name. They have so gathered in churches throughout this land, and in Christian churches throughout the entire world. And repentance and forgiveness is preached to all nations, even as the Lord Jesus commanded. It was not by chance that this day was set aside primarily as a day of worship, for it was the day in which darkness and death were vanquished; and the strong Son of God rose victorious from the grave. The first day of the week we call Sunday. In the ancient cultures it was known as the day of the Sun.

And our Savior said to the disciples, and also to us: "Why are you troubled, and why do questionings rise in your hearts. For thus it is written that Christ should suffer, and on the third day rise from the dead," offering repentance and forgiveness to all nations—that by believing in his name, ours can be a life that is everlasting. It was on the first day of the week, at the early dawn, when the stone was rolled away; and the women beheld the angel of the resurrection, and Christ our Lord had risen from the grave. Amen.

KINGDOM TIDE INTERLUDE

CHAPTER 16

THE MOUMENTAL MEANING

In a military cemetery on one of the Pacific islands, we can see row upon row of white crosses. Immediately we are struck with the vast number of men who lie under the soil of this volcanic ash. The palms sway gently in the wind, and the stillness of peace reveres this ground. It is only when we look upon the seemingly endless row of crosses that we catch a glimpse of the massive cost in human lives squandered here. These crosses stand as symbols of human sacrifice. The picture painted on the mind is impressive, although not always lasting. In this vast scepter of death, the individual has lost his personal identity. The small, white, uniform crosses are all alike.

Few of the men buried here are ever remembered, and when they died their names were merely added to growing list of statistics. They did not choose to lie here. They had no territorial ambitions. The bands were not playing or the flags flying when they died. Nor did they pass away in a blaze of glory, yet they lie here, long since dead. Today the people of America will be seen flocking to our national cemeteries with flowers in their arms. In millions of homes, memories, and hearts, the dead will live once again for a brief moment. They will not be physically seen, but their presence will be felt by our spirits. Memorial Day is upon us.

From The Threshold Of Heaven

The meaning of Memorial Day is commemorative, serving to preserve in remembrance our dead. We remember them because they are a part of us, because they still live in the depths of our hearts. In remembrance of them we are made to realize that no human individual stands alone, or lives solely by his own wisdom and might. Behind the frail fabric of life there is a unifying spirit of mind and power that links man to man and generation to generation. To our dead, to those who have gone before us, we owe more than we can possibly imagine. The freedom we enjoy, the beliefs we hold dear, and what we do rests largely on what others have sacrificed for, done, and thought before us. While it is true that the memorial of our dead is commemorative, and makes their names linger in our thoughts in the nobility of their aspirations, it is more than this.

The monumental meaning of Memorial Day lies in recognition of what these did while they lived. There are countless numbers of men who made very little impression on their generation. There are others who are remembered, if they are remembered at all, in infamy, whose names have become by-words for all that is mean and debased. But there are others whose names stand out in the history of world as beacons of courage, nobility, and self-sacrifice for all generation. We hold these men in honor. We tell our children about their exploits, hoping to instill in them their high aspirations and noble traits of character.

What have our dead left us? Some have left us a strong concept of personal freedom, of democracy, and an elective form of government. Others have opened new doors of human service in their conquests of disease and advancement in the field of medicine. The music we best enjoy comes from the pen of composers long since dead. We read their books, sing their songs, obey their laws, intone their prayers, and mediate on the sacred Scriptures they helped preserved. Those long since dead carved out nation out of a vast wilderness, won its independence, led it to its present destiny, and preserved it free. For this we especially honor them this day. And in remembrance of them we pray that we may preserve and carry out their ideals and fulfill the visions for which they gave their lives.

Lest we forget, Memorial Day was born during the Civil War. While the struggle was going on in other parts of the country, flowers were being placed on the graves of those who died in both the gray and blue uniforms on the battle field of Gettysburg. Today we remember and honor all who have donned their country's uniform and have died in her defense. What they died for faced, in my generation, a more serious challenge and graver threat than ever before. The forces that opposed our way of life, and our system of government, were impelled by a philosophy of satanic madness. They were an avowed, ungodly group of ruthless and barbaric atheists. They exterminated millions in a blood bath of unparallel proportions and enslaved countless of millions more in the satellite nations. They ruled, where they had sovereignty, by armed force, brutality, and terror. In this orbit of terror, the common people were free only to fear and live out their days in dread. For nearly fifty years we were engaged in a gigantic struggle to determine which of the two opposing systems of government and society would survive. Our dead who engaged in this struggle did not see the issue resolved in our favor. And yet, we feel and believe that our dead have not died in vain. We shall retain the freedom, the government, and the way of life our dead preserved for us.

But our dead have given us even more. To them we owe the depth of knowledge of our spiritual realities, our present concept of God, and our current visions of heaven. There was one who having lived in glory with the Father, descended to earth and became identified with us. Having done so, in the power of God's redeeming Spirit, he gave a new birth to all who acknowledged him as Savior and Lord. Through the sacrifice of himself on one of these crossed, Christ our Lord restored humanity to the bosom of the Father. But Jesus Christ, Son of God and Savior of the world does not lie beneath the soil of this earth. Before the Cross of Christ stands an empty tomb. Our faith became a reality because the grave could not hold captive Jesus Christ, the prophet of Galilee. It was not possible for death to hold him. God did not allow his holy one to see corruption, but raising him to heavens heights, crowned him with glory, honor, power, dominion, and majesty.

The meaning this has for Memorial Day is that our Lord's victory over death can enable us to transcend the present and be instilled with expectation for the future. Hope does not stop at the vast number of monuments or with the dead they represent. The white crosses that fill our national cemeteries need not be the sad reminders of those passed on to a dark, unknown place; but rather, they are monumental symbols of what shall yet be. That which we have come to know as death is not the end. Although our lives may appear to be but a brief visit on the surface of eternity, we shall not pass away into oblivion. When God created man and joined his body to the soul, man became eternal in soul and spirit. Some of us will find this difficult to accept or even unbelievable. In an article by the rocket scientist, Dr. Wernher Von Braun he wrote wrote.

> Many people seem to feel that science has somehow made religious ideas untimely or old-fashioned. But I think that science has a real surprise for the skeptics. Science, for instance, tells us that nothing in nature, not even the tiniest particle, can disappear without a trace. Nature does not know extinction. All it knows is transformation. Now if God applies this fundamental principal to the most minute and insignificant parts of his universe, doesn't it make sense to believe that he applies it also to the human soul.

> Dr. Von Braun concludes.
> Everything science has taught me, and continues to teach me, strengthens my belief in the continuity of our spiritual existence after death. Nothing disappears without a trace. (Excerpt from Guidepost. Used with permission)

What we call death is not extinction, but rather transformation to a higher phase of life. Listen to the hope, the power, and the strength which St. Paul puts into his words.

> Lo! I tell you a mystery. We shall not all sleep, but we shall be changed, in a moment, in the twinkling of an eye, at the last trumpet. For the trumpet will sound, and the dead will be raised imperishable, and we shall be changed. For this perishable nature must put on the imperishable, and this mortal nature must put on immortality...then shall it come

to pass the saying which is written, Death is swallowed up in victory. (1 Cor 15:51-54RSV)

The crosses which symbolize death do not mark the end. We need not recall Memorial Day with heavy hearts, though we may have tears for the love of those who have gone before. Nor shall we make it a day of sadness and self-pity. Have we not ever wondered why a cross marks the resting place of our dead? It is—because the cross is the symbol of the Christian faith, a symbol of hope and future glory. The Cross says: "Because our Savior lives, we too shall live." The bones of our beloved dead may lie under a carpet of green, but their spirits soar in heaven's heights, subject to the call of him who is all power and might, and who has swallowed up death in victory. Against the background of the small, white, uniform crosses, stands the cross of Christ our Lord. And it is for us the symbol of the day that shall never end.

Of course, there are times when we wish that the day would draw to a close. For a moment we may have lost the vision of heaven, and the thought of death may hold us captive. At such times we ought to recall that Jesus Christ came to set the captives free. We acknowledge that there is an awful loneliness and stillness about death. What I can say is this: if we have known Jesus Christ this side of the grave; if we believe that he has redeemed us and delivered us from the power of sin and death, then we shall be ushered into his presence when the dawn of faith shall have come for us. To claim the great Galilean as our Lord will give meaning to our days on earth, and set in the future a life beyond the moment we know as death; and it shall be a life of wondrous glory. Amen.

CHAPTER 17

THE MAJESTY OF THE AWAKENING CHRIST

There is a common disability that affects most of us, whether we are the man working in the fields, the scientist in his laboratory, or a mother dealing with the agony of a sick child. We suffer from the human inclination to doubt our Savior's ability and power. Yet, when we look to the Lord Jesus for strength to pass through a crisis, or for patience to see us through period of recovery, there ought not to be all that much difficulty. Christ is of God. He is all in all. He has come as our Redeemer, and has promised us his power and his presence.

Ours is an age of wonders and marvels in the fields of communications, electronics, and medicine. A microchip, no bigger than one half inch square, can store vast amounts of data, and we can recall it in an instant. All these things we see, hear, and operate every day, and they have in them the components of physical properties.

The marvel and wonder of our religion, which we have in the Lord Jesus, belong to another dimension. For us, faith in Christ is still the substance of things hoped for, the conviction of things not seen. We know that at times it is difficult to believe, when everything seems to run counter to traditional teachings, that our faith is not always strong, and that the conceptual belief we retain may be imperfect. But there is no sin or moral wrong here. It is only blatant unbelief that precludes the healing touch of grace. The disciples were in a boat with the Lord Jesus, and a strange thing occurred. Their expression of trust, and faith, in his power was so weak, that it was hardly apparent at all. The Lord Jesus was moved to ask them, "Where is your faith?" (Luke 8:25).

The Calm, the Storm, the Peace.

It had been a long day for the Lord Jesus, a day of teaching and proclaiming the glad tidings of the Kingdom of heaven; and the press of the multitude had been upon him all day. While he viewed the people with compassion, the men closest to him were in need of further instruction. They remained perplexed at the spiritual meaning of the parables. The Master of Galilee knew it was time to draw off from the multitude, and to be alone with his disciples. He instructed them to go over to the other side of the lake. And as they entered the boat to cross over, not one of them gave attention to the signs of the times, to the shifting wind, the harbinger of a coming storm. On the far horizon, hidden behind a thunderhead, a storm was brewing that would fall upon the lake in the fury of all its elements. In the boat, they felt secure, for the lake was calm and all was at peace.

When they pushed off from the shore, Jesus settled in the stern of the ship and lay down to sleep. All seemed at rest, all appeared at peace, for all was quiet. Having assumed a body like unto his brethren, the Savior's need for sleep and rest grew out of his true humanity. As the grace of God appeared in Christ Jesus, bringing salvation to all men, the revelation of his humanity would be followed by the revelation of our Lord's power and divinity.

For a time the boat moved across the waters quietly, but the clouds began to gather, and the sky began to darken. Then of a sudden, before they were aware what had occurred, the storm was upon them and the wind raged over the waters.

The waves rose higher and higher, tossing the ship about. And all the while, the Lord Jesus, Master of oceans, and skies, and seas, lay fast asleep in the stern of the ship. The danger increased rapidly. The ship began to fill with water, and the disciples feared greatly. Although in the presence of the Lord Jesus, his disciples feared because they did not know what manner of man their Master might be. Although perfect faith may cast out fear, the disciples had not advanced that far in their perception of spiritual realities or in their knowledge of the Lord Jesus. Unable to control their anxiety, their fear increased, taking full possession of them. They awakened Jesus and cried out to him: "Save us, Lord, for we perish."

We wonder whether the disciples had hoped, more then they had believed in our Lord's power, when they awakened him with their plea. True, they had turned to the Lord Jesus and became his disciples, but they had yet much to learn. They did not understand the Savior's fullness as the only begotten of the Father. But on this occasion, God would make known to them the majesty and fullness of Christ—the occasion of the storm would bring out the full revelation of our Lord's power and divinity, and of who he was. Their Master, Christ, and our Redeemer, made in fashion as a man; nevertheless, had the form and power of the Most High God. Our Lord's divine personality would confirm that Jesus was of the very God of creation. Still, for the disciples, as well as for us, there was needed the coming of the Holy Spirit to reveal the mystery of the Savior's person. We believe this incident is included in Scripture, that all might see that as the Master of the elements, our Lord controlled the forces of nature by the word of his power.

The exercise of our Savior's power occurred, like when the Lord God in ancient times parted the Red Sea and made a way for the redeemed to pass through. The Lord Jesus, when awakened by the cries of his disciples, "rebuked the wind and the sea." And the winds and the waves obeyed his voice; for all things are Christ's.

He is all in all; and by our Lord Jesus all things were made that were made. The elements, being created, are his creatures and subject to his will—even when raging in the fury of the storm. The Lord Jesus commanded the seas, "Peace. Be still."

Immediately the wind ceased its fury and the trouble waters abated, and the sea was calmed and at peace. Startled, the disciples were filled with wonder. "Who then is this, that even the winds and seas obey his voice?" Who, indeed! Then, the Lord Jesus asked his disciples: "Why are you afraid; O men of little faith." We trust that their faith was not entirely gone, only weak.

Christ is All in all.

> For he has made known to us [through the Spirit] in all wisdom and insight the mystery of his will, according to his purpose which he set forth in Christ...to unite [in Christ] all things in heaven and all things on earth. (Eph 1:9-10RSV)

The concept of our Savior being all in all is the very center of all our believing. With Christ as Lord, there really can be no insurmountable difficulty, for all is his. And there is no failure of his grace, when we address our prayers to the Lord Jesus. As Christ was present with his disciples in that ship in the middle of the tossing waves, so shall he be with us in our personal struggles and changing fortunes of life. Life can be very fragile; our fortunes can change over night, and in an instant the peace we have known may be shattered. A home destroyed by fire, a severe personal injury, or a love one taken by a sudden illness, all these are real incidents of every day life, and we are not immune to any one of them.

Our saving grace is that our Savior is with us, and that in every painful experience he is there awaiting our call. Our faith may be lame, and we may not have the ability to penetrate all the mysteries of the Kingdom of heaven; nevertheless, though we may be struggling with some personal problem, we can still look to Jesus as Savior and Lord. We can still pray for help and guidance; for the one thing we must do is to appeal to his mercy, and believe in his ability to be of aid. The prayer of Simon Peter, in that moment in the fury of the storm, came from all of us, brief as it may have been. Its inclusion in Scripture was meant for our comfort and assurance: "Save us Lord, for we perish."

There may be occasions when, we like the disciples as they pushed off in the boat, may be unable to predict what lies ahead of us, unable to see the gathering storm clouds on the far horizon. Into each of our lives, the day of trouble will eventually come. It is then that we ought to turn our thoughts to our religious beliefs. The expression of our religion is found in the incidents of faith, hope, and love. Our hope is in knowing to whom we can turn, and in knowing that he is able to hear, draw near, and answer our prayers.

Jesus Christ, the Master of oceans, and skies, and seas is much more than a Savior from sin and death. To us, he is all in all, and will remain so through all the years ahead. With him as our Redeemer, there ought to be no difficulty that cannot be overcome: since he is all in all, all is his. And all may be ours because he has promised us his power and his presence.

The Majesty of the Awakening Christ.

Yet, there was much more, which the Spirit revealed—in what manner of Savior we have in him who calmed the troubled sea and abated the fury of the storm. When the Lord Jesus slept in the stern of the ship, recovering strength for his body, his humanity was revealed side by side with his divine nature. When the frantic appeal for help came; the sleeping Son of man *was surpassed by the Majesty of the Awakening Christ*—rebuking the wind, commanding the elements, and displaying his divine dominion over the sea. The calm sea was eclipsed by the fury of the storm, and of a sudden, all was overwhelmed by the majesty of the awakening Christ in dominion and power.

The disciples stood in awe at the revelation of our Lord's divine power: this was their Savior and Lord, the Teacher come from God. What a glorious thought this is—that his triumph over sin, suffering, and death; and all that love revealed on the cross, can be experienced by those who have turned to the Lord Jesus. Though the centuries may separate us from that day when the Son of God calmed the troubled sea, his invitation remains the same and is extended to us. Our doubts, and our lame faith mixed with fear and reverence, may cause us to think our cry is too faint to be heard.

But this is only an appearance. We need only cast our cares on him, and he has promised to hear and to be our Savior at all times. We need only bring to the foreground of consciousness our Lord's power, ability, and willingness to be our strong support; and Christ will emerge in the full response of his power, grace, and glory. Let us remember always, all is Christ's, and we are his; and he is our. This is the Savior I would leave with you, he who is all in all; and whom I would have you experience through an unwavering faith in him.

Prayer.

> Eternal Father and gracious Lord, grant us the blessings of thy grace; and remember once again, we pray thee, that at times our hands of faith may be very lame. But send even now thy Holy Spirit to touch our hearts that we may know that thou art ours, and we are thine. Amen.

CHAPTER 18

GOD WHO MADE THE WORLD

For hundreds of years men wondered what God might be like, the incidents of his character and the nature of his dealing with men and women. They had read stories of his appearance on Mount Sinai, where the thunder was heard exceedingly loud, and the lightening lit up the heights, and the smoke rose to the heavens as from a furnace. But there was death shooting forth out of those rocks for any, man or beast that might approach and touch the mountain. Those who were about the camp could only stand off and look up at the heights, and glance toward the heavens. Perhaps the ancient ones had been wrong; perhaps they had misread the signs. Could God be like Zeus in Greek mythology, over all the lesser deities, coming with a thunderbolt in his hand, or like Thor, the god of war, mighty and majestic in all his power?

The images of divinity carved in stone and marble, in gold and silver, were far too many and so diverse in figure and form that the average heart, the active mind, and seekers after God turned away in despair. And yet, the most skilled artisans, the profoundest minds, and the teachers of morals had given their portrayals, their philosophies, and their opinions about the nature of deity. And none were in harmony with each other. Men gazed at the constellations, at the marvels of the expanding universe, and wondered like our present day astronomers, whether the solution to the mystery of godliness might not lie out there among the furthest galaxy, and forever beyond their reach. No, said St. Paul, the resolution of man's eternal quest is much nearer than that: for it is "Through faith {that} we understand that the worlds were framed by the word of God, so that things which are seen were made of things which do not appear" (Hebrews 11:3).

What God is Like.

> God who made the world and everything in it, being the Lord of heaven and earth, does not live in shrines made by men...as though he needed anything, since he himself gives to all men life and breath and everything. And he made from one every nation of men to live on the face of the earth...that they should seek God, in hope that they might...find him. {We} ought not to think that deity is like gold or silver, or stone, a representation by the art and imagination of men... he commands all men everywhere to repent, because he has fixed a day on which he will judge the world in righteousness by [Jesus Christ] whom he has appointed, and of this he has given assurance to all men by raising him from the dead. (Acts 17:24-31).

God, whom we contemplate as the Father of our Lord Jesus, is the Lord of heaven and earth, the creator of the ends of the universe. How could men possibly conceive that The Almighty might be contained in temples made by men, or housed in shrines as though he were in want and had need of food and drink? Must he be appeased for compliance to human will? Absolutely not. Much rather, he is the benevolent Father who gave life and breath to all men, and provided for their subsistence through the providence of his creation.

We can understand the confusion of the ancient ones, and the difficulty of the modern mind in giving assent to the God and Father of our Lord Jesus Christ. Yet, God in his wisdom must have known that men were in need of the revelation of his character and his way of dealing with men. We are led to believe that if man were not to make God in his own image, then he must have a revelation about the nature of God from the threshold of heaven. It is the intellectual process of our perception and mental faculty that compels us to reason that only God can reveal God, his nature, his Christ, his way of dealing with men—and his requirement of righteousness.

It is revealed, and it is through revelation that we understand that The Almighty delivered Israel from the house of bondage in Egypt, brought them safely through the desert and the Red Sea to Mount Sinai. There, to sanctify them unto himself, and gave them through Moses, the law. God is also the Father of our Lord Jesus Christ in whom God's grace was revealed, bringing salvation to all men. This is the essence of revelation, to reveal that which was hidden, obscure, or unknown. Revelation sheds light and drives away the darkness, giving knowledge, meaning, and direction for human life.

From his revelation of Christ, St. Paul presented to the people of his time the concept of God as the sole divine power that created the worlds, and the race of men in his own image. He proclaimed this God is he who provided them with all that was required to sustain life, that they might be led to worship him in gratitude and praise. But St. Paul's presentation was refused by the wise men of Athens.

The Nature of God's Dealing With Men.

In the opening chapter of his letter to the church in Rome, Paul laid out the way of God's relationship with men in three massive strokes: (1) God requires righteousness from all men; (2) since men of themselves are unable to attain such rectitude of life, righteousness may be obtained as a saving gift of God's grace through faith in Christ Jesus; (3) God will exercise judgment on all unrighteousness of men. The moral philosophers might have agreed that righteousness would be an acceptable attribute of any concept of God they might imagine. They might have also agreed that in that great judgment hall beyond the closing of time, a good man had nothing to fear from a righteous judge.

The objection of the world to St. Paul's conceptual presentation was based on what the apostle used to establish the certitude of his belief. The disposition of the final tribunal would be conducted by the Lord Jesus. Of this tribunal, *God had given "assurance to all men by raising him (Christ) from the dead."* When Paul said that men ought to repent, he meant they should live a righteous life, and turn to faith in Christ Jesus.

The Nature of Believing.

The Gospel that St. Paul presented to a civilization already steeped on the road to decline, he alleged to have received by revelation of Jesus Christ. His Evangel was rejected in Athens because the most enlightened men of that age thought it a thing incredible, that a trained mind could entertain the concept of a God who raised the dead. Implied in their expression of contempt for Paul's message was included the refusal to give assent to the God who made the world.

Again we ascertain this truth: mere knowledge, intellectual attainment, and academic achievement alone can never turn an individual to repentance or to the Lord Jesus. And although no human mind or all of them together, are capable of legislating for reality, men continue to suppress knowledge of God as creator—and his requirement of righteousness. Somewhere along the span of life, whether early or late, one must be touched with spiritual perception, a desire to know God's love and the grace of our Lord Jesus Christ. The soul must be awakened to that life which is nurtured from above, and the heart must be gently moved. We acknowledge that we are speaking of things unseen; yet, we are touching on things hoped for, and looking for the inclination of the human heart to the conviction of God who made the worlds.

Well, if God made us, created the heavens and the earth, endowed us with the breath of life, and shed abroad his love in our hearts through the Holy Spirit which was given us; then, we can reason about him, about life and death, and about our Lord Jesus Christ. We can do so when our minds turn to God in affection, when we petition for pardoning grace, and open our hearts to the influence of his presence. For the mind that seeks to know God, there must be equanimity of mind and spirit, and it is essential that the individual turn to the Lord God with the whole heart.

Has it not always been true, that when we believe upon hearing the Gospel, it is because the Holy Spirit has touched our hearts and made us receptive to the word of the Lord? Or when we come to accept the church's teachings, it is because we have been nurtured in her life, carried in her bosom, had our soul affected, and assented with a willing mind. And although we may not always see ourselves in the act of perception, it is nonetheless true: that it is "Through faith that we understand that the worlds were framed by the word of God, so that the things which are seen were made of things which do not appear."

God's Gift of Righteousness.

Though the Lord God has appointed a day in which he shall judge the world in righteousness, he has also offered men and women a new and living way, through whom the requirement of righteousness may be obtained. Our Savior's Gospel of the Kingdom of heaven begins with a turning to the Lord Jesus, through which we become the recipients of God's saving way of forgiveness—as a gift of God's grace. Through our Father's mercy, come absolution, faith, and reception into the Kingdom. The soul attains new life by the grace of God, by love emanating from above, by the Holy Spirit, and through faith nurtured in the hearts of men and women. And faith in believing hearts brings with it the righteousness of God, which is in Christ Jesus our Lord.

How simple, how beautiful, and how marvelous is the nature of God's dealing with those who trust the destiny of their souls to his care. Simple words these: grace, truth, spirit, and love, all products of God's benevolent concern for men and women. As we abide in his love, God who made the worlds will hold our lives in Christ Jesus. And he will bring us into his eternal presence on the day of his glorious appearing. Amen.

SECOND ORDER OF ADVENT

CHAPTER 19

ADVENT PAST

First Sunday in Advent.

The expectation of the advent season centers on the anniversary of the coming of the Lord Jesus as the promised Redeemer. In the thoughts of our hearts, and in the imagination of our minds, we will walk in the fellowship of the Spirit. We visit the time of advent past, when in the greatness of his power God wrought the marvel of the ages, his incarnation in the baby Jesus. The divine birth came as the realization of the hope, which grew out of God's dealing with men, in the days when the kingdom of Israel was falling out of existence. Jeremiah, one of the prophets of those times, wrote:

> Behold, the days come, saith the Lord, that I will perform that good thing which I have promised....In those days I will cause the Branch of righteousness to grow up into David... and this is the name wherewith he shall be called, the Lord our Righteousness. (Jeremiah 33:14-16)

The Past Promise Realized.

In the past promised of God realized, we see the grandeur and immensity of the providence of God. Though the nation of ancient Israel seemed forsaken, its power vastly diminished, and its population drastically reduced, Jeremiah wrote of the encounter he experienced with The Almighty. The encounter came to assure Jeremiah of the certainty of God's word—the certainty of its fulfillment:

> The Lord hath appeared of old unto me, saying, I have loved thee with an everlasting love; therefore with lovingkindness have I drawn thee to me. (Jeremiah 33:3)

In commemorating the birth of the Christ child, our memories awaken. As our memories awaken, we think back to the meaning of these events, that so deeply touch us, and we turn our thoughts to the workings of God. Thoughts of the past mingle with thoughts of the present. We think of the loved ones we know and have known. We think on those whom we shall put on our Christmas list. We contemplate the tree we shall purchase for the living room, and reflect on the seasonal gatherings we have enjoyed before. We get ready to commemorate that day, when the decree went out from August Caesar in the advent season long since past. And we think on the message of the prophets that told of the good things to come. Justin Martyr wrote.

> In the book of the prophets, we find Jesus, our Christ, foretold as coming; born of a virgin, growing up into man's estate, healing every disease and every sickness, raising the dead, being hated, unrecognized, crucified, and dying and rising again, ascending into heaven, being and being called the Son of God through the prophetic spirit, which announced beforehand the things that would come to past. (Justin Martyr, <u>First Apology</u>,
> Anti-Necian Fathers, Vol. I)

From The Threshold Of Heaven

The things which were foretold were the provisions of divine mercy for the human race, which God wrought in the birth of his Son, Christ Jesus. The words of the prophet came to a people deeply disturbed, divided, and far from the paths of home. His words came as a message of the coming one. In his advent, the coming one would serve as a revealer of God, and of his concern for his people. The people must have thought back, when the Lord God had moved among them, working his wonders of healing and provision. Surely, they thought about their deliverance from the land of Egypt, God's parting of the Red Sea and about his presence in a cloud over the Tabernacle. Could they have forgotten about the pillar of fire that guided them by night, or the cloud that led them by day? The words of the prophet Jeremiah touched their heartstrings and stirred the memories of God's past dealings with them.

As we look back in the pages of our memory, we can never think of Christmas without also thinking of shepherds tending their sheep. We think about wise men approaching from the east, following a star. Images are awakened of Mary, the mother of the baby Jesus, of Joseph, the manger, and of the inn which had no room. With hearts that beat a little faster, we contemplate the birth of our Savior in a stable, born a child, and yet a king. The good thing which God gave—how we look back to that. And how, also, we look forward to those things, which "eye hath not seen, nor have ears heard," which the Lord has reserved for those that love his appearing. The advent season overflows with the sense of goodness, with the affection of love, and with the spirit of generosity. Advent moves with feelings that seem to bind us one to another. There is a gentle up-lifting in the atmosphere of the season; and it began from a promise made in ages long since past.

For a world lost in selfishness and sin, the revelation came, when God said, no longer will men be without a visible Redeemer and manifestation of my care. Although the Lord Jesus came in the form of an infant, he grew to man's estate. And the world came to know that in Christ Jesus, the grace of God appeared, bringing salvation to all men. Nor did the wonder of God's working end there. From that advent past in old Judea, streams of glory and spiritual treasures have continued to flow over the far reaches of the earth. The light of

God's visitation has shone, driving away the darkness of the centuries, and the world was unable to put it out.

God's Righteousness.

> In those days I will cause the Branch of Righteousness to grow up unto David... [and] Judah shall be saved.

Jeremiah characterized the moral nature of the promised Redeemer: his conduct would be virtuous, morally right, and equitable. When Joseph went with Mary to be enrolled and came to the city of Bethlehem, it was because he was of the house and lineage of David. It was not only a righteous act, but also an act which fulfilled that which the prophets had written about the place of the Christchild's birth. And as the representative of righteousness, the Lord Jesus came destined to rule in the hearts of his people. And when God gave his Son for the life of his people, and the Son became identified with his people. God also gave them the attribute of righteousness through his Son.

Although destine to rule in his Kingdom, the Savior's province was not like the earthly grandeur of David's former dominion. However much David's kingdom was filled with splendor and power, it was still of this world, and its nature earthly. The Savior's realm was in righteousness, and in peace, and in the dominion of the Spirit. His Kingdom came in the form of the Kingdom of Heaven. And as Jesus ministered to the multitude, his work appeared as dealings which led to their ultimate good. And the people's ultimate good led to the redemption which we have in Christ Jesus. Our Savior's ministry in the Kingdom of heaven began in that long since advent past.

Today, we still look to that first advent, now past, when Jesus came born of a virgin, growing up to man's estate, healing every disease of body and every sickness of soul, raising the dead, being hated, unrecognized, crucified, dying and rising again after the power of an endless life; ascending to heaven, being, and being called the Son of God. During the presence of God incarnate on earth, who healed the ills of the body, our Lord also attended the needs of the soul—and the need righteousness that flowed like a never ending stream over the length and breadth of the land.

The Past is not all Past.

In this season of wonder and mystery, we must not think that all that has gone before is only of yesterday. Nor are we to be dismayed in thinking that we may have left a great deal behind. Much of yesterday moves with us in the stream of life and becomes a part of us. The past, and the past promises of God, are the building blocks upon which we build our lives, and our faith. It is for those who have known the kindness of God to make the most of past heavenly encounters; and to make the most of the gifts that have been given to us. In our deepest thoughts, and close to our hearts, we keep the past, the memories, and the promise of good things alive. And yet, all this was more than a dream, for our Lord's coming was an invitation to receive him, for he is our righteousness. This is his special gift to each of us. And even though millions may have refused him—for he would not win by compulsion—still, millions more have turned to him, won by his love. There is a gentle persuasion that attends the season of advent.

> Because I have loved thee, said the Lord, with an everlasting love; therefore with lovingkindness have I drawn thee to myself.
> (Jeremiah 31:3)

As the Spirit of God touches us softly, and moves the heart, we are drawn to the Lord Jesus. We may wonder at the thought of God's having loved us, written in days gone by. How could the creator of this vast universe love us personally, or even think of us individually? And what is there about us that would make God love us? We have done nothing great. We have never given our body and soul to some great cause. And who is actually righteous among us? No one.

Yet within the mystery of our faith, and in the wonder of God's grace, we are not to worry about the workings of God. In the beauty and simplicity of the Gospel, if we have known the Son, we will be loved of the Father. And in so doing, we have acknowledged him as God—and Christ Jesus becomes the Lord our Righteousness. Though it may have come to us from the far distant past, the grace of God is ever present; and it moves into the future, because advent comes with faith, hope, and love, and our soul's redemption. Amen.

CHAPTER 20

ADVENT PRESENT

Second Sunday in Advent.

The human race needed the first advent, which is now past, which signified the coming of our Lord Jesus. Men's hearts were failing them for fear and desperation. The noble expectations once proclaimed by the best of the world's religious had long since fallen into oblivion, and there was little but duty to up-lift and guide ones course in life. And yet, every city had its gods and temples of worship. But the night had already fallen on the people of the Roman Empire, with despair fast closing in upon them. There was an absence of hope, and desire had died like a declining shadow. Then, and now, it is only the Lord Christ that can dispel the enclosing twilight and flood the plain with light. He can lead us to the Father, to the noble, the just, and to love of the good.

The Present Age.

Yesterday is neither past nor prologue, because it is full with meaning and rich with instruction. The manifestations of God's concern in human history are the foundations for faith, for those who seek affinity with God. Even though the present age is one of wonder, scientific marvel, and space exploration, the enduring values revealed in the course of history move with us into the current age.

From The Threshold Of Heaven

Along with reaching into the vast expanse of the universe, seeking out its glories and splendors, we have also delved into the micro cosmos of the atom. Computer technology is being outdated every other month, and our accumulation of information has become massive. The incidents of wealth and comfort have never been more apparent. While poverty is still wide spread among us, the balance of the weight is on the side of an affluent society. Things have been made easy for most of us.

There is an actual historical drama concerning two men who had to choose between a kingdom and the women they married. Jerome Bonaparte, the youngest brother of Napoleon, was married to an American woman named Betsy Patterson. The emperor told his brother that he could never obtain the throne he intended for him, as long as he remained married to this American woman. Jerome Bonaparte abandoned his wife and became king of Westphalia.

Then, there was Prime Minister, Stanley Baldwin, having been born in sin, and having before him the precedent of Napoleon who slaughtered half the population of Europe, made an identical demand on Edward VIII. Edward VIII was already king of England. Baldwin demanded of Edward VIII, that either he separate from Wallis Simpson, his American love, or abdicate the throne. Scarcely any one has heard about Jerome Bonaparte, but in 1936, and even today, the whole world knows about the Duke and Duchess of Windsor. Edward's choice set the whole world to wonder. He must have been touched with grace. He gave up the throne and an empire for the woman he loved. As a prince of a fellow, Edward VIII made a monumental sacrifice. This was, and will ever remain, the greatest love story of the twentieth century.

Questions arise. If we have become relatively affluent, and if things have been made easy for us, have we become, or are we becoming a soft generation? Have we lost, or do we still possess the strength of character to make a sacrifice? Do we retain the ability to endure hardship for a noble cause? If it should be required of us, can we give up some of the things that make life easy for us, simply to stand for the right, the just, and the good? If it would cost us dearly, can we still say no to that which is wrong, and no, also to the wrong means?

Our Lord held his redemptive mission to be dearer than life, and suffered death on a cross to bring us closer to God. What will a man give in exchange for his soul? In the novel, The Tenth Man, by Graham Green, thirty men imprisoned by the Gestapo in France must choose between life and death. Three must die, and the choice well be made by lot. Chavel, a wealthy man, watches as two men with the marked lots are taken out to die. Only the third, doomed lot remains, and now Chavel must choose. Fearful, he fingers one lot, lets it drop, and takes another. He has chosen the last marked lot and will be taken out to die.

Distraught by fear, Chavel is beside himself. He offers one hundred francs to any one who will take his place, but no one takes up his offer. Desperate now, he offers all he has: his money, land, and home. What shall a man give in exchange for his life? All he has. A poor man wishing to leave something for his family, accepts Chavel's offer and sacrificed himself for his family. The rich man gave all he possessed to save his life, while the poor man gave his life to save his family. Could any of us do that? I wonder. Are there those among us who can still make a sacrifice?

Loss of Awareness.

Are we aware of the issues that hang in the balance? Are we aware of the consequences of the choices that we make? Do we realize that most individuals have lost knowledge of the significance of Christian symbols? How many actually know that purple is the accepted color for advent? In a society moving at a rapid pace, we sense a slow and steady loss of spiritual awareness. A dull insensitivity appears to be creeping over us, and many are in danger of losing the sense of the love of God. We are in danger of losing, also, the sense of the nearness of Christ, and what his presence in our lives implies.

This loss of awareness was not an overnight process. Rarely does loss of spiritual awareness appear self-evident. It comes upon people as though it occurred in the still of the night, as though it came in the serenity of sleep. It occurs without the clamor of noise, without our being conscious of it, and without any sense of pain. But its true significance is spiritual death; and an encircling darkness lurks in the background of our society. And I believe—that it is to dispel this foreboding—that the advent season is come upon us, overshadowed by grace, by love, and by the hovering of the Holy Spirit.

Advent Present.

In the benevolence of our heavenly Father, the coming again of the advent season always drives away the deepening shadows.

The Lord, whom you seek, shall suddenly come into his temple, even the messenger of the covenant, in whom you delight. (Malachi 3:1)

Justin Martyr wrote that it is in the nature of God to reveal what is going to come to pass; and Scripture teaches that God intervened at the proper time in the course of human history. We understand time through the order of events that measure its passing. In time, we have the rise and fall of nations, the revolutions of societies, the expanse of communications, and the birth and growth of our own nation. The present time is truly appropriate for the coming again, of the advent season. And with its coming, advent brings with it the aura of spiritual things. We sense again the presence of God the Father. And in the anniversary of the birth of the Lord Jesus, God reveals his compassion for men and women.

The compelling spirit of advent lies in its revelation of love, compassion, and concern; and in the thought that God was willing to send us his Son. Though by the world's standard our society is affluent, and through our religious convictions we are empowered to endure hardship for a good cause. We can still say no to that which is wrong, and even no to the wrong means. We can look again to the wonders of grace, love, and things unseen—all of which are awakened in us by the coming of the Lord Jesus during the season of advent present.

CHAPTER 21

ADVENT FUTURE

Third Sunday in Advent.

Advent was meant to be a season of joy and of peace and good will among the nations of the world, as well as among individuals. It was intended to usher in a time of peace and safety; and instead, today, there is horror, and strife, and blood letting about the face of the globe. Advent, announced by the voice of an angel, told about the coming of the Savior of the human race. But as we view the current world scene, it is difficult to imagine a Kingdom of peace and righteousness the world over, or the rule of a gentle spirit in the hearts of men. We are continually reminded of the wars in Africa and in the Balkans, the deadly strife in the Middle East, and terror in our own cities. To the natural eye, it seems that our present civilization is irredeemable, that peace and tranquility could never have been anything more than a dream.

We wonder whether permanent peace was not an illusion, a thing imagined in the mind of mystics and political idealists. It is no more nearer to reality now than it was at the end of the First World War, or at the end of the Second World War, or at the conclusion of the several subsequent conflicts in which our nation has engaged. The war in the Gulf, in which we led in the order of battle, was to rescue an autocracy from the clutches of a tyranny, but we were told that our national interests were at stake. No pretense was made of "making the world safe for democracy." As it turned out, the greatest danger which American troops faced, possibly, was 'friendly fire," which is just as deadly as enemy fire. And yet, in this advent season, world peace seems more of an illusion than ever. Now we are engaged in a war on terror—but we shy away from the terrorists in Palestine.

NATO appears weak and ineffective. The peace keepers of the United Nations are abused, cajoled, detained, and shot by whosoever will. And it seems that the very purpose for which these international organizations were created to secure, they are utterly unable to execute. Little wonder that expectation has turned to futility, that member nations mistrust each other, and that the salvation of the human race will never be found where irresolution has become a trade mark, and indecision a way of life. We wonder what can be accomplished, where moral weakness and spiritual paralysis preclude the bearing of the real cost in pain and suffering that must be paid if peace is to be secured.

The process, by which peace has been sought, has been nothing short of appeasement of the Serbs, the Muslims, the Palestinians or any other entity that has expressed an interest in the outcome of the wrath and slaughter of innocents. The Balkan conflict appears to have ended in despair for one people, and the reward of greed for the others. Not because the victors were more determined, more self-sacrificing, or more upright and deserving, but because they were more savage and ruthless, cast disdain on the United Nations, heaped contempt on NATO; and because they broke every bond that ever existed between man and man. Then, is all hope precluded for the human race? We think not.

Advent Brings Hope.

> Surely the people is grass; the grass withereth, the flower fadeth; yet the word of our God shall stand forever. (Isaiah 40:8)

We trust that Christian people, the world over, can still be included in that segment of the population, which has not placed hope for peace and redemption solely on this earth. While the prospects of salvation for the world appear obscured in darkness, restrained by selfishness, and held in check by parochial national ambitions, our civilization has survived similar periods of gloom and despair. And it seems likely that our world will emerged from the war on terror not totally unscathed, but surely tainted. We trust that we fall in line with the majority, when we hold that our way of life, and government, are worth fighting for, and worthy of dying for if need be. And ultimately for us, our hope is in God who quickeneth the dead and calleth the things that are not as though they were.

We are of a fleeting, passing nature, and our life is no more than a breath in the existence of time. But him to whom we look in the season of advent, and who appeared in history as the coming one, is of an imperishable nature; and his presence is the revelation of his glory and grace. Neither our Savior's Kingdom nor his Spirit is of this world. And with Christ Jesus there is no illusion, no deception, and no promises that fail with the coming of the night or with the passing of time.

Although the Gospel of the Messenger of the Covenant has been with us for a long time, the presence of our Lord works miracles of transformation and wonders of renewal in human lives day in and day out. This season, which brings the remembrance of grace that can cleanse the human heart, of forgiveness that absolves our fears and guilt, announces the one true hope of the world: the Lord Jesus Christ. The issue is what do we trust in? On whom do we place our expectations? And what do we believe? Is not God's coming incarnate to dwell with his people of eternal significance?

The Spiritual Aura and Force of Advent.

The tendency of many people who consider themselves knowledgeable, up to date in things that matter, and cultured, is to turn away from the God of creation and God of salvation. They took away from the concept of divine intervention and the destiny of providence. They suppress thoughts of the supernatural and down play spiritual expression and emotion. When this attitude of mind, and disposition of heart, invade the Kingdom of heaven; the result is a deadening of the spiritual life of the church, and the spiritual life of her members. We have passed through a period, where religious thought divorced itself from the God, who became incarnate in Jesus Christ; and whose mission it was to reconcile men and women to God and to each other—by his sacrifice on the cross. Yet, those who disclaim an atoning and saving Christ, and refuse to acknowledge the God who intervenes supernaturally in human lives, have lost the essence of Christianity and the spiritual significance of advent.

The ultimate realities of the Christian religion are that God shed abroad his love in our hearts through the Holy Spirit which was given us; the presence of God in Jesus Christ; and Christ's presence with his people. These are the supreme incidents of divine intervention in human lives, and they are supernatural, and they are essentially spiritual. When our Lord said that his Kingdom was not of this world, he implied that we ought not to be so tied to the physical phenomena, that we permit it to be controlling in the expression of our religious life and thought.

However much the ministry of the Church may serve as the saving grace of our society, and serves to hold in check the encroachment of evil and moral decay—the advent season reminds us that the Christian religion is supernatural, inner, and spiritual. God is a Spirit, and we worship him through our spirits in gratitude and praise.

Advent Looks to the Future.

Our hope is in the Lord God, and hope in us is the expectation that leads us to look to the future. We confess that we and the world have been created, that our Lord's compassion is of infinite capacity and concern for the future of our world; *and that what has been created can be recreated.* The Spirit, which is God's presence with his people, can always empower the church, and along with her, her people to continuous renewal. Revival and renewal, of whatever sort, always begin with a new religious impulse. And the greatest religious impulse ever given to the human race came in the first advent season with the birth of the Lord Jesus.

Our Christian literature records our Savior's ministry and teaching, his atoning death and resurrection. His word, which God declared through his prophet Isaiah to be eternal, discloses our Lord's continuing presence in the Spirit with his people. God's word also revealed the coming of our Lord's Second Advent, to consummate the triumph of his church in the New Heaven and New Earth. And of this, the first advent was a foreshadowing. Advent means the coming, and when we speak of Advent Future, we refer to the Second Advent of our Lord Jesus Christ:

> For our commonwealth is in heaven; from whence also we we look for the Savior, the Lord Jesus Christ. (Phil 3:20)

For us, in our time, it is well to remember that the guardian Spirit of this season is the same Spirit that was active in creation and in the conception of our Lord Jesus. The Spirit comes with all the God given power to transform and renew; and God who sent the Spirit upon us is still the supreme arbitrator of history. We look to the future, to save the future, and to redeem it from sin, selfishness, and greed. We move into the future, compelled by the force of time; yet, knowing that time itself is but a created mode of human existence. We do not move alone, for God is with us. And peace and good will are worthy objectives of the faith, to which we assent in our minds and harbor in our hearts. Though in our journey, like the grass, we wither and fade away, yet the word of God shall stand for ever; and to be absent from the body, is to be present with the Lord.

CHAPTER 22

THE MIRACLE OF ADVENT

Fourth Sunday in Advent.

One of the blessings of advent lies, in that the coming of the Lord Jesus, God revealed his care for the people of the earth. Before advent's revelation on the nature of God's dealing with men and women, hope and desire seemed suppressed. And without these emotions stirring life, there remains little reason to plan, dream, or reason to look too far ahead. For some individuals, every day comes as dull, drab, and disheartening. Existence within such a milieu appears aimless. With other individuals, the desperate, escape is sought in extreme, and at times, in deadly diversions. But such was never the creator's design. Even after our original parents fell through disobedience in paradise, the Lord God set before them the way of hope and faith. God promised to send humanity a Redeemer; and the people were to set their prospects for the future on this promise. The advent of the Lord Jesus came as the most promising grounds of assurance ever given to the human race.

St. Paul wrote that those who have known the Lord Jesus ought not to live and think like those individuals without hope. The absence of all prospects for the future is an attribute of the lost and disillusioned. But we have not so learned the Lord Jesus.

The Lord God in the midst of thee is mighty; he will save, he will rejoice over thee with joy; he will rest in his love, he will joy over thee with singing. (Zephaniah 3:17)

The Hope Which Comes With Advent.

I made a home visit to a young man who suffered from a mental disorder. Physically, he appeared quite fit; he was strong, tall, and had a pleasant appearance. But he was unable to read, because the letters appeared backward and up side down to him. He also suffered from seizures, and when an attack came upon him, he was in danger of biting his tongue or the sides of his mouth. In addition, he was mentally retarded and had a form of epilepsy. As I spoke to his mother, she expressed the thought: "You always pray for a miracle, but you don't hold much hope."

In spite of insurmountable difficulties, she retained a small spark of hope; and it stemmed from her love for her disabled son. Because of his disability, the young man was unable to pray, or otherwise help himself. And his mother had to pray for him—and hope for him. Though she confessed she did not hold out much expectation of success, through her petition, she reached out in faith and prayed. Prayer tunes our thoughts to God. In the face of physical barriers, nearly impossible to overcome, the mother intoned the request that the course of her son's illness be reversed. Because she loved her son, she prayed; because she had faith, she prayed, even though the prospect that her request would be granted were dim.

The grace of our Savior's compassion is that he does not turn away from our imperfect knowledge, or from our imperfect hope. The dimly burning wick of faith was a thing precious to the Lord Jesus. Our Savior always responds to the longing of the soul, to the broken heart, and to the despairing. And he has not forgotten those who are physically or mentally ill. Some day in the future, we may find ourselves on a sick bed. Or we may be compelled to stand by and see a loved one suffer from a lingering and irreversible illness; and medical science can do no more then relieve the pain. As we watch and wait, our unspoken thoughts echo the words of the disabled son's mother: "You pray for a miracle." Still, we wonder because we do not hold out much hope.

Nevertheless, because of our faith in the promises of God and in the Lord Christ Jesus, we are not like those without hope. Advent means that our Savior's coming is in a special way. His presence awakens hope in the human heart. And although our trust may not be great, the Lord will respond to the longing of the soul. And he comes to those who look to him for grace to help in their hour of need.

Advent Brings the Savior Near.

In these days, when we celebrate the anniversary of his coming, the Lord Jesus draws near to help and to redeem. If we are attentive to the signs in the heavens, and to our own inner feelings—in the remembrance of days of shepherds and wise men—we sense the presence of the Spirit. It is an awareness of the nearness of the Lord Jesus. In pain, in sorrow, and in death he has promised to be our helper; and we need only reach out to him in our thoughts and in our prayers. In an issue of Guide Posts, Maxine Arthur told this story:

> It was near the end of a long afternoon at the County Fair. The children were tried and parents cross. I was wondering if being a parent was worthwhile. Then I noticed a woman on the merry-go-rouind. She stood alone as the carousel whirled...But she did not seem to be enjoying herself. When the carousel stopped, she got off and walked away. At a short distance, she stopped and burst into tears. She wept for the child to whom she had promised that ride, and who was no longer there to receive it. I felt tears sting my eyes as I looked down at my children. I thanked God for the richness in my life that he had reminded me of. God came very close to me that day, speaking to me in whispers by showing me the sorrow in the life of another. (From Guide Posts. Used by permission)

On this occasion, the Lord Jesus drew near Maxine Arthur, reminding her of the gifts he had given her, through the loss that another human being had sustained. And Maxine Arthur responded in gratitude to the Lord God. The Savior's presence had removed the negative thoughts that had been pulling her down.

There come times when we can do no more than pray and hope. And it is possible that had we not suffered pain or loss, we may not have turned our thoughts to God. But advent is the season when the soul awakens to spiritual realities, when we awaken to the wonder and miracle of the Savior's coming. We can turn from the disturbing incidents of life. We can look to him whose ministry came in simplicity and humility; and who came to call a people unto himself. We can turn our thoughts to the Lord Christ Jesus whose Spirit pervades every day of the advent season. If we would, we can reach out and touch him. And if we do so, we can regain our desires and expectations for the future. The birth of the baby Jesus reminds us that advent is also a time of new beginnings. And hope is born anew with each new beginning.

Advent is a Time for Prayer.

The wonder and spiritual aura of advent tell us that this is a season for prayer. Prayer is a valid religious experience. Prayer puts our soul in touch with the great unseen Father of our spirits, because it opens our lives to the presence of the Spirit. And this, we truly need. We need not pray for a miracle, but only for a sense of the presence. For it is the Spirit of God that gives inner strength and enhances human life. For heartaches and struggles, for the toils and tribulations of life, fortitude alone is never enough. We need something much more—we need the grace of the living God. We may receive it through prayer.

In the season of advent, we pray also for world peace. Though it is an annual occurrence, the advent season has lost none of its influence for peace and good will. This truth remains: good will among men and peace on earth always seem a possibility during the Christmas season. And while among the nations, peace appears to recede beyond the far horizon, it can be a different matter for the human soul. We know that the Savior's coming is with grace and compassion, and we are bidden to draw near in expectation. We await his touch. We seek his peace. We lift up our souls to his Spirit. And as the Savior's presence is upon us, the night is stilled. The elements are at rest; and his peace will have come into our lives.

CHAPTER 23

THIS WILL BE A SIGN FOR YOU
(Christmas)

Our story is found in St. Luke's narrative of our Savior's birth. As he revealed the mystery of the greatest event in history, which occurred on the first Christmas day, Luke wrote about angels, shepherds, and about good news of great joy.

The Situation.

For the appearance of the promised Redeemer, the trusting hearts of the people had waited. And though expectation may have grown dim for many, they clung to the hope and comfort of the Scriptures. The long years were silent ones. It had been ages since a prophetic voice had spoken for God, and truly there must have been a hunger for the word of the Lord. Seekers had search about, yet both heaven and earth held their peace. The years stretched into decades, and the decades expanded into centuries, and there was only the quiet voice of the wind, like a stillness unto God. Some doubtful individuals expressed the opinion that, perhaps, the creator of heaven and earth had forgotten. Was it possible that God, in forgetting his people, no longer loved them or cared for them? No. That could not have been possible, for they read in the synagogues every Sabbath, from the law and the prophets, where it was written.

> But now thus saith the Lord that created thee, O Jacob, and he that formed you, O Israel, Fear Not: for I have redeemed you. I have called you by name; and you are mine. When you pass through the waters I will be you; and through the rivers, they shall not overwhelm you; when you walk through the fire you shall not be burned; and neither shall the flame kindle upon you.
>
> For I am the Lord your God, the Holy One of Israel, your Savior; I gave Egypt as a ransom for you...because you are precious in in my sight and honored, and I have loved you. (Isaiah 43:1-4)

God had not forgotten; it was only that for faith to mature, expectancy should grow in the human heart. Men and women must desire the Lord, his grace, mercy, and righteousness; and when this desire was full, the people would be ready. That was the moment, when God manifested his grace in the birth of his Son, Christ the Lord.

News From Angels.

When the revelation of God's purpose came, it was received from the voice of angels. Those humble shepherds were simple men, doing the things of every day life in their vocation. They were caring for their flocks, keeping watch, waiting in the fields for the coming of the day, when the shadows and dangers of the night would pass away. They were watching under the stars, gazing up at the vast expanse of the universe, perhaps, looking for a sign. That was when the heavenly vision appeared, and it came upon them suddenly.

> And the angel said unto them, be not afraid; for behold, I bring you good news of great joy which shall be to all people; for unto you is born this day in the city of David, a Savior who is Christ the Lord. (Luke 2:10-11)

At long last a voice from the eternal sanctuary had broken the silence. The Lord God had forgotten neither his promise, nor the manifestation of his love. The waiting was over. On this day, the proclamation announced that the long-expected Redeemer and Savior had come, descended to earth from the threshold of heaven. But the good news from the angel is also for our generation, of the Saviors coming, of his birth, and of the grace of God revealed in Christ the Lord. The embodiment of this love came from the heart of God, for all ages, for all people, for us and to our posterity for ever.

This Will be a Sign for You.

But where would they find him, and how would they know him of whom the angels had spoken? And the angel continued.

> And this will be a sign for you: you will find a babe wrapped in swaddling clothes and lying in a manger.
> (Luke 2:12)

Once their fears were allayed, the shepherds believed and accepted the message, nothing doubting; though they wondered in awe, reverence, and in spiritual humility. Who were they that grace and glory should come so near to them? They were those who were poor in the things that the world counted as dear. These simple folks, with believing hearts, could only look to the advent of the Kingdom of righteousness. Yet to such as these, the news of the angels was given. And has it not ever been so? God, working through ordinary human beings always seems to confound the wise.

To the shepherds was given this sign by which they would know him of whom the angels spoke. They were not to look for a great king, or a mighty man of valor. Instead, the shepherds were to look for an infant, a baby newly born, in swaddling clothes, and lying in a manger. By these signs which indicated the simplicity and poverty of the child's birth, the shepherds would find and know him who was born Christ the Lord. Taking the message of the angels to heart, they went quickly to find the holy baby. And by the prompting of the Spirit, instinctively they were aware that their hopes, dreams, and the realization of God's love lay there. All lay there in the life of this newly born child. And even today, we, like those ancient men of the fields, also wonder, and marvel, at this great thing which God has wrought. Yes, we wonder that on the feeble heart throb of this infant life, God, creator of heaven and earth, hung the salvation of the world.

This was our Heavenly Father's commitment to the human race, the fulfillment of all the promises. The holy child came as the eternal hope of Israel and the heavenly Father's visitation with the people of earth. And while there may have been a great unseen company of witnesses round about, there was no visible care to watch over the child's safety, no housing other than a stable and a manger. And is it not so, also with us? On what slender thread may hang the continued life of our family, or the life of the church, but on the tiny heart-beat of every newly born child? With God, we need no visible means of support, other than faith. Without faith we have nothing, but in believing we have everything: God, Christ, and the Holy Spirit come along side to help. The narrative tells us.

> And when they saw it, they made known the saying concerning this child.

How could they help it? How could they not have made known the saying concerning this child, the sayings which they had received from the angel—and for which they had waited so long?

The Wonder of It.

> And all who heard it wondered at what the shepherds had told them. (Luke 2:18)

News from angels? This in itself was a wonder. But it was the message that caused the people to wonder—a Savior for all the people, who was Christ the Lord.

A Savior who came born as a baby in the form of human flesh such as we, and yet born the Son of God. Little wonder that when the people heard the shepherds tell their story, they marveled. But had they known what Simeon knew, their wonderment would have known no bounds. Simeon knew that this holy child was the realization of everything; of all the signs, types, and symbols; of the Ark of the Covenant, the Shewbread, the Rod of Aaron, the seven-branched Candlesticks, and the Golden Altar from which incense ascended upward to heaven. This was the promised Christ of God, and the end of the law for righteousness. He brought redemption to all who would turn to him. And Simeon knew, because it came to him by revelation, that this child now held in his arms was the very visitation of God. And though now a little baby in his arms, this was he of whom Moses in the law, and the prophets had written. With perfect peace of heart, and in tranquility of soul, Simeon responded to the Epiphany of grace which he held in his arms:

Lord, now lettest thou thy servant depart in peace, according to thy word; for mine eyes have seen thy salvation. (Luke 2:29-30)

The shepherds, star, wise men, and the manger will live in our memories; and we trust also in our hearts. And so too will the angel that brought the glad tidings. This Christmas we recalled all those wonderful events which occurred long ago; and we would never want their significance to be lost in all the activity of the Christmas season. But when all is said and done, these, and even the swaddling clothes and stable were but signs. They were signs that Christ had already come, and apart from the Lord Jesus, they have no meaning. The miracle of Christmas is the birth of the Christ child who brought the visitation of God into the world. And in the Christmas season, thoughts about the Christ child fill our minds, as our memories turn to the climax of the advent season.

But we must do more, because mere memory is not nearly enough. We must move to a personal encounter with the Lord Jesus. This strange and wonderful image of the invisible God must live in our hearts, and this must be an experience that our soul has gone through. Here alone is where the real wonder of his grace begins; and for this, Christ was born. He is the Christ of God, the Savior of advent, and of all times. He can still work the works of God, and continues to do so in every human soul that gives him room.

We have made known to you once again the sayings concerning the Savior, and we would also make known to you the wonders of his coming. Should you really desire to know Jesus, let him come to you with his love and gentle Spirit; and in your heart, soul, and mind you will know him and the wonders of his grace. And from the bosom of The Almighty, who has not forgotten either his promise, or his love for those who seek his presence, this will have been a sign for you in this advent season.

THE SECOND ORDER OF LENT

CHAPTER 24

ASH WEDNESDAY

SEEKING THE PRESENCE

As we move through the countryside and streets of the city, past shops, schools, and residential areas, we see the things that occupy people's lives and ambitions. They tell us, and their close friends, that their next home will be larger and in an upgraded neighborhood. Next year they will take that trip to Europe, they will need a new compact disk player shortly, and the drapes in the living room need to be replaced. Then, there are the family problems. There always seems to be a difficulty, an illness, an unforeseen event with someone in the family; and the taxes have to be paid. Sometimes we feel that we may be pushing too hard and too fast, and we have been doing it all year long. We sense that we are not in harmony with ourselves, with the world, and with God. While we may not always thank God for Friday, we can be thankful for today, Ash Wednesday, which marks the beginning of the forty days of lent.

> Seek the Lord while he may be found, call upon him while he is near; let the wicked forsake his way, and the unrighteous man his thoughts; and let him return to the Lord, that he may have mercy upon him, and to our God for he will abundantly pardon. (Isaiah 55:6-7RSV)

Ash Wednesday and the Nature of Lent.

Ashes used in a religious service, bore witness to the ancient ceremony of purification. What the ashes signified, gave the name of Ash Wednesday to the day which marks the beginning of the lenten season. It was not so much the outward act of the ashes sprinkled over the worshipper that was the central religious meaning, but what the ashes represented, a penitential disposition of heart. Then, as now, it was the internal state of the individual that made him receptive to the love of God, and to the cleansing grace of forgiveness. Of this, ashes were the sign. We look upon these days as a time of devotion, prayer, and care of the soul. In the season of lent, we seek the presence of The Eternal, and we would like to be worthy of approaching his presence.

The intent is to turn our thoughts away from the things that clutter our lives and so occupy our minds that we scarcely give time to our religious life. In lent, we look to prayer, fasting, and self-denial as expressions of our desire to obey the Lord's command to "take up our cross and follow" him. Coming as an impelling voice from apostolic times, it is a heartfelt desire "to enter into the fellowship of the Savior's suffering;" that we may be near him, identified with him, and share in the burden of the world's redemption.

In the spirit of the lenten season, ideally, we give up things, tone down worldly festivities, and turn to worship that we might draw nearer to the essence of our faith. Fasting and self-denial are the outward acts of the penitential attitude. Praise and gratitude are acts of worship that spring from our inner nature. Prayer inclines the soul to the Father of our spirits, is submissive to his Spirit, and brings obedience to his will. At no period in the church year are prayer, fasting, and self-denial so much a characteristic of the Kingdom of heaven—and of the individual members of its commonwealth, as in the forty day period of lent, from Ash Wednesday to Easter Sunday. We seek to be a people prepared, a little more worthy of God's presence, that his grace may enhance our spiritual life.

Estrangement is From the Heart.

What have the things of the world, which seem to occupy our lives, done to us? How has preoccupation with success and ambition affected us? And do we have reason enough to be concerned about our state of mind, as well as our well-being? Indeed we do. What we sense is a lessening in the depth of our religious life, a fading away of those images, concepts, and feelings that once moved us so acutely. The estrangement is felt in the heart. This sense of alienation comes with the thought of having removed ourselves from the guidance of our Lord's pastoral care.

At the conclusion of his work entitled, "Critique of Practical Reason," Immanuel Kant wrote: "Two things fill the mind with ever-increasing wonder... the starry heavens above me, and the moral law within me." We do not need to be told that we have sinned and fallen short of what God intended us to be. But we seek relief from the heat of the day and the press of the storm. We acknowledge that we have been so involved in busy work, that we have neglected the inner part of our being. We confess that we have not given enough attention to our religious life or to the cultivation of our soul. The days of lent were meant to bring us again, with ever-increasing wonder, to the realization that God, who hung the starry heavens above us, and who placed the imprint of his hand within us, loves us, and cares what happens to us. Nor is he so infinitely removed from the affairs of men, that we could never reach him, or look to him, or address him in our prayers.

Though our aims and thoughts may remain unspoken, during the season of lent, we seek for the avenue into the presence of The Eternal. What occupies our time and attention from Ash Wednesday to Easter is precisely this. And in our religious sentiments, initiated with fasting, prayer, and self-denial, we seek to overcome the sense of estrangement in heart from things of the spiritual realm. We wish to make up that which we feel is lacking in the life of the soul. In this pilgrim journey, we are encouraged through the aid and comfort of the Scriptures; and in seeking the Lord while he may be found.

For the mountains may depart and the hills be removed, but my steadfast love shall not depart from you, and my covenant of peace shall not be removed, says the Lord who has compassion on you. (Isaiah 54:10RSV)

God shed abroad his love in our hearts through his Spirit, which moves through all the events of the lenten season. We seek his presence through the things which we do in the outward acts of religious meaning. We look for an exercise of faith, a movement from the impulse of the soul directed toward heavenly things. God's love for us is sure, holding fast, even though the elements of creation may be in convulsion. His promise of peace shall not be removed from us by the going down of the sun, or the changing scenes of nature. And as day follows day, and season follows season, we are encouraged in our pilgrimage toward Calvary; and we will call upon the Lord while he is near.

The Spirit of Lent Fills the Longing of the Soul.

As we move further into the forty days of fasting, self-denial, and prayer our souls will begin to stir and our religious consciousness will have been awakened. We will sense a tugging at our souls, a gentle pulling of our heartstrings toward the heavenly place, taking us away from the things of earth. In seeking the Lord, worldly means and wicked ways will be forsaken. This becomes part of the lenten journey. The ways of the unrighteous shall be far removed from us, because we know that the unrighteous shall not inherit the Kingdom of heaven. We seek a closer affinity to the things of the Spirit world and to the Lord God, that he may have mercy upon us.

The gentle, suffering spirit of the Lenten season tells us that the Christ of God draws near, and we wait that moment when we become aware of our Savior's presence. We seek inward understanding of the mystery of Christ revealed to us, and experienced by us. We seek and desire, as the longing of our souls is aroused, hoping, and waiting, "Until the Spirit is poured over us from on high" (Isaiah 32:15), and God's righteousness settles down upon us;

for righteousness from God will lead to peace, quietness, and trust for ever.

What will we have done with our little ways of fasting, self-denial, and prayer? We will have been trusting to the word of promise—seek and you shall find, knock and it shall be opened unto you. We have been seeking, in ways that have been given us, the presence of God, and of his Christ. We know that our religious life will be better for it, our souls touched, and our hearts at peace. We move to that moment when the veil of the temple is torn in twain, opening up the entrance to the heavenly sanctuary, where our prayers and supplications have ascended.

The journey is never long; and all too soon we will have moved beyond Passion Sunday, and find ourselves in the upper room on Maundy Thursday. From there, with those who were closest to the Master, he retreated to the Garden of prayer. From the Garden the mob of the chief priest took Christ and delivered him up for trial. And on Good Friday, the cross was lifted up. Holy Saturday passed quietly, as though the guardian angels knew that already on Good Friday, the veil had been torn in twain and heaven's door was opened wide. All, now, may seek the Lord God and call upon him; for he will have mercy upon us; and in his compassion, he will abundantly pardon.

CHAPTER 25

FORESHADOWING THE RESURRECTION

First Sunday in Lent.

In our transition through the season of lent, we draw near to the Lord Jesus as he moves toward the climax of his mission. During these slowly lengthening days, we encounter a prelude of the Savior's final triumph over the forces of evil, followed by the prologue of humility and glory. We pass through the night of betrayal to the hour when the Lord proclaimed, "My time is at hand." The Cross hovers in the background. In the events of Good Friday, Darkness and evil appear to have won, while Holy Saturday is hushed in apparent despair. Then, suddenly, all the wonder and victory of Easter breaks forth in its glorious resurrection morning. And in the immortal words of our ancient church father, Ploycarp: "Jesus Christ has changed sunset to sunrise," and he has done so for ever.

As a token of the efficacy of our belief in Christ, we begin with the raising of Jairus' daughter. Against the actual death of a little girl, our Lord Jesus revealed the certitude of our religious convictions—in so far as they are centered in him. In this act of compassion, we see the energy of life, which our Lord Jesus called out in those that turned to him as Lord.

Jairus, a man who had turned to the Lord Jesus, was a ruler of the synagogue. And as we turn to the Lord Jesus in our loss and sorrow, Jairus was encouraged in the Way of Christ through the loss of his little daughter. To us, this may occur through personal injury, a disturbance in a family relationship, or through the terminal illness of a loved one. In passing through these hurtful incidents of life, fortitude and personal courage are never sufficient to sustain us. We will discover how often we turn to the patience and comfort of the Scriptures. We look for the hand of God.

Jairus had an only daughter, 12 years of age who became gravely ill. Nothing seemed to have been of aid; and the child did not get better, but worse and seemed to be dying. The father had reached the end of all human resources, and now to whom could he turn? Jairus had a friend, the Lord Jesus. As his friend, he may have witnessed the work and healing ministry of the Lord Jesus as the Savior had moved among the people. The Lord's compassion and ability made a lasting impression on Jairus. And as one of the rulers of the synagogue, he had heard Jesus speak in this house of worship, and his soul had been deeply moved. In his hour of need, Jairus knew to whom he would go. St. Luke narrates the story of the raising of Jairus' daughter in his Gospel.

> And there came a man named Jairus, who was a ruler of the synagogue; and falling at Jesus' feet he besought him to come to his house, for he had an only daughter...and she was dying...
>
> While he was still speaking, a man from the ruler's house came and said, "Your daughter is dead; do not trouble the Master any more." But Jesus on hearing this, answered him, "Do not fear; only believe, and she shall be well."...
>
> When he came to the house...he said: "Do not weep; for she is not dead, but sleeping." And they laughed at him, knowing that she was dead. But taking her by the hand he called, saying, "Child arise." And her spirit returned, and she got up at once... And her parents were amazed. (Luke 8:41-46)

Only Believe.

Believing in the sovereignty of God, we also believe no outcome of God's grace is a meaningless occurrence. There is divine purpose in each. And although this purpose may be hidden from us, it is not so to him who works all things after the counsel of his will. While all may seem an orderly sequence of events; nevertheless, God's providence is always at work. Our Lord had overheard the messenger from the ruler's house tell him his daughter was dead, and that Jairus should trouble the Master no further. The Lord Jesus was not disturbed by the news of the girl's death. Instead, he turned to Jairus, his friend, and said: "Fear not; only believe."

To Jairus and the people about him, the girl was truly dead; and his religious convictions were weighed, when informed of his daughter's death. But the ruler of the synagogue held fast to his faith in Christ, which included belief in our Lord's ability and his power over death. He had turned to the Lord Jesus firm in his faith. He did so even though members of the multitude laughed at the thought that Christ could raise the dead. Still, this has always been the way of those who do not believe in the divine Christ. When it was all over, and his daughter brought back to life, Jairus knew that the divine Savior had vanquished the power of death, and had brought life and immortality to light.

This is an age that finds it difficult to believe that Christ could heal at a word, or that he could still the elements of a raging sea by just his voice, "Peace: Be Still." Some individuals find it more difficult still to believe that the Lord Jesus could raise one from the sleep of death. But this was precisely what Jairus had to believe, as he walked by the side of the Savior, while they made their way to his deceased's daughter bedside.

A Prelude to the Resurrection.

When he came to girl's bedside, the Lord Jesus took her by the hand, spoke to her, and brought her back to life. The narrative says that her spirit returned, and that she got up at once. In the heart of Jairus, the Lord Jesus had changed sunset to sunrise. His faith in

Christ had been tested, and Jairus was not found wanting. Unknown to this ruler of the synagogue, who had turned to the Lord Jesus, in raising his daughter from death, Christ had given Jairus a prelude of the Savior's own resurrection.

As the events of the first lenten season were leading to the Cross and the crowds beginning to melt away, the faith of the disciples would also be tested. Although their faith may have wavered, in the end it was refined and also held firm. We can imagine their anxiety, their doubts, as the Cross hovered menacingly in the background. For the wonder of Easter's resurrection lay hid behind the silent clouds of Holy Saturday. Like Jairus, and like the disciples, as our souls lean to things eternal, we will discover the wonder and simplicity of the efficacy of our trust in Christ. This religious experience, acquiring certitude in our faith, may occur to any individual; and it may occur through the pain of personal suffering and sorrow—and, also, through joy in the Holy Spirit.

Each of us continues to move to our final destiny, as did the disciples of our Lord. There came for them the tragedy of the night of betrayal and the crucifixion on Good Friday. But there had to be the Cross before the emergence of the resurrection, and the Savior's ascension before the coming of the Holy Spirit.

Perhaps, there may be a cross that we have to carry. There may be a heartbreaking disappointment for us, as there was for the Lord, when Judas Iscariot walked out of the upper room. We may sustain a disturbance of a family relationship; and even the loss of a loved one through a terminal illness. And while our faith will be called out, and tested, it need not falter or fail. We ought to fear no incident, no tragedy, not even death itself. This we know, and our convictions affirm, that Christ is also Lord of eternal life; and that his alone is the power of the resurrection.

CHAPTER 26

THE PRELUDE OF HUMILITY AND GLORY

Second Sunday in Lent.

At the Passover meal, the Lord Jesus knew that within a few days, his mission on earth would be over. At the conclusion of the Last Supper, when having instituted the sacrament of Holy Communion, he rose from the table. He took a towel, and poured water in a basin. Then he did a thing which puzzled the disciples, and astounded Simon Peter. Christ began to wash the disciples' feet. Then he wiped them dry with the towel. Simon Peter thought the task unbecoming for the leader of his religious movement. Peter refused to put his Lord in a position of servitude.

Afterward, when Peter submitted to the ministration of Christ, the Savior explained what he had done: "I have given you an example, that you should do as I have done...for a servant is not greater than his master" (John 13:15-16). The Lord Jesus demonstrated that his ministry came as one of service and sacrifice. If they in the upper room with him were to be men of the Kingdom, they would have to serve the Lord in meekness and humility. But the little drama in the upper room also prepared them for something more important in their future ministry—knowledge in the way of God's dealings with men. And it pointed to our Lord's journey into the valley of humiliation. Christ must pass through this valley in order to fulfill all that was written by the prophets. Our Lord's humility, his unassertive demeanor and humbleness of spirit, with which he carried out his mission, is ascribed in Scripture as one of the reasons why God raised him up from the dead, and exalted him to a position of honor and praise:

> For being found in human form he humbled himself and became obedient unto death, even the death of a cross. Therefore God has highly exalted him and bestowed on him the name which is above every name. (Philippians 2:8RSV)

In the season of lent, in which almost every event is filled with sacred meaning, it is well to remind ourselves that God does some of his greatest work through ordinary individuals. He works best through men and women of the Kingdom obedient to his will, unassertive in their bearing, and who like the Lord Jesus, with humbleness of spirit look to him for guidance.

God Does Not Work Through Overbearing Individuals.

The main characteristics of our Lord's personality were meekness and gentleness, together with sympathetic understanding for an individual's circumstances. Simon Peter recognized that his Master engaged in a humble service, when he washed the disciples' feet. Still, Christ did it as an act of humble courtesy. This humble act served as a preparation of what was to come, his humility in the court of the high priest, and at the Roman tribunal before Pontius Pilate. The Lord Jesus made no move to defend himself from the accusations of the chief priests and scribes.

His whole bearing displayed an absence of pride. Notwithstanding his silence, Christ, standing before the judgment seat of the world and the force of his personality, were such, that the Roman procurator could find no wrong in him. Although the presence appeared unassuming, the witness of his ministry; his healing, the miracle of changing the water into wine, the raising of Jairus's daughter from death, and the feeding of the five thousand, was that God was with him and working through him. And the testimony of the disciples affirmed that the Spirit of God was in and about the Lord Jesus.

When the children of Israel were still in bondage, Moses, the son of Pharaoh's daughter, came upon them at their labor. He encountered an Egyptian taskmaster abusing a Hebrew, and he decided to intervene on behalf of the slave. As a result of his intervention, the Egyptian taskmaster was slain. Though Moses had sided with the people of Israel, his offices of aid were rejected by the individual he sought to help. Scripture reveals that Moses supposed that they would have understood that God meant to deliver them by his hand. But they did not. Why? The reason was that Moses had not submitted the question to God for resolution. He did not seek divine guidance in the matter. Nor had he made a heart-surrender of his life to God. He had come on like a proud Egyptian prince, far too aggressive and self-assertive. What had actually occurred?

Moses had been overbearing, ruthless, and committed murder. When his rash act of homicide became known, he was compelled to flee for his life into the wilderness of Midian. His rash act had accomplished nothing. While it was God's purpose to visit his people and to deliver them from bondage in Egypt, he was not going to work through a proud overbearing individual. He would not do so then, and he will not do so now.

The Lord Jesus had given his disciples a lesson in service and humbleness of spirit. It was a lesson Moses learned through forty years of tending sheep, privation, and waiting. But when Moses answered the call of God from the burning bush, and returned to lead his people out of Egypt, he was marked as a man of meekness and of a humble spirit. Moses became an effective instrument in the purpose of God, when like the deliverer he typified, he assumed our Lord's humility and unassertive demeanor.

When We are Unassuming, God Works.

Why did the Lord Jesus think his personal example so necessary that it was among the last teachings, which he left with his disciples during their final hours together? It was because within a few days his physical presence would no longer be with the disciples. The course of lent, which led to the cross and tomb, was far too advance to be reversed. And God's purpose to reconcile all things in Christ was immutable. If the disciples were to carry out their great commission, God's purpose and Spirit would have to work through them.

It is difficult, if not impossible, for the grace of God to be seen in a selfish individual who places his own interest before the interest of another—in the work of the Kingdom of heaven. No service for the church will be fruitful, when there is lack of sympathy for those with whom we deal and the absence of esteem for them in their own right. The effectiveness of our Lord's ministry and sacrifice was that in humbleness of spirit, he typified obedience to the divine will. And in Christ's bearing of meekness and gentleness, the manifestation of God's Spirit was not obscured. Hence, the divine purpose was realized through the Lord Jesus.

With the physical presence of the Lord Jesus no longer with the disciples, they would have to look to the presence of God's Spirit guiding them and working through them. When the Lord God deigns to dwell with an individual, God's presence is in his Spirit:

For thus says the high and lofty One who inhabits eternity, whose name is Holy: I dwell in a high and holy place, and also with him who is of a contrite and humble spirit. (Isaiah 57:15RSV)

In the upper room, when Christ washed the disciples' feet, he was leading them to one of the prerequisites of character so necessary for them, when it came time for them to take on the leadership in the early Church. For the proper growth of the Church, the question was, has the Spirit of Christ fallen on the subsequent leaders of the Church? The development of the apostolic Church affirms that it did.

God has Exalted Him.

Because Christ faithfully discharged his mission—and fulfilled all righteousness—God exalted him to a position of praise and honor. The Lenten season ends with the Cross of Good Friday, fowled by the silence of Holy Saturday. Then came the glad morning of the resurrection. And later, the resurrection was followed by the ascension of our Lord to the heavenly sanctuary. The glorification of the Lord Jesus was far removed from the upper room, where he had girded himself with a towel and washed the disciples' feet. But the lesson he taught them has as much meaning for us as it did for them.

The Spirit of God still moves over the broad reaches of the land. He still looks for men and women attentive to his calling, obedient to the divine will, and doers for the Kingdom of heaven. In the cause of righteousness, in the struggle of good against evil, and in the fight of the right against wrong, God's Spirit still does his best work through ordinary human beings. God works through those, who with humility of heart and humbleness of spirit, look to him for guidance, for strength, and for the sustenance of their spiritual life.

CHAPTER 27

THIRTY PIECES OF SILVER

Third Sunday in Lent.

Within the circle of the immediate followers of Jesus, there was self-sacrifice, self-indulgence, and denial. When Judas Iscariot left the upper room, his subsequent acts made his name synonymous with treachery and betrayal. There was nothing heroic about his conduct; and we can imagine the self-searching his desertion caused in the other disciples. His departure was but another sorrow for the Savior to bear. All these things were part of lent; its meaning, its sorrow, its suffering, and its progress, while the threatening clouds hung overhead. The plots of the high priest, the searching of the scribes, and the questions of the lawyers with double meaning, all moved in one direction—wherewith to accuse innocent blood, how to condemn the uncondemned, the man Christ Jesus approved of God and anointed with the Holy Spirit.

Judas, on the inside, and counted as a member of the disciples, may have hidden his disappointment for some time. The reign of spirit and truth was not going to add materially to his wealth. He was unable to postpone immediate gratification for any good that was future and unseen. For the treachery he contemplated, thirty pieces of silver appeared adequate:

Then one of the twelve, who was called Judas Iscariot, went to the chief priest and said: "What will you give me if I deliver him to you?" And they paid him thirty pieces of silver. (Matt 26:14-15RSV)

When our Lord was gathered about the table at The Last Supper, he said, "Truly, I say unto you, one of you shall betray me." Judas asked, "Master, is it I?" The Lord responded, "You have said it." Some hours later that same evening at the Mount of Olives, Judas came, leading a vulgar mob, and with a kiss which was more like a token of death, he betrayed his Master. Because he had done no wrong, "the chief priest and the whole council sought false testimony against Jesus, that they might put him to death" (Matt 26:59RSV):

When Judas...saw that he was condemned, he...brought back the thirty pieces of silver and said: "I have betrayed innocent blood." But they despised him saying: "See to it yourself." And he departed; and went and hanged himself. (Matt 27:3RSV)

Analysis of the Transaction.

An analysis of the transaction proves instructive. The betrayer was one of our Lord's disciples who had inside information. He knew the details of the ministry's activities; where they met, slept, and went to worship; and where the Master went to pray in seclusion. He also had in his possession the common purse, and perhaps he appreciated the value of money. He sold into the hands of evil men one whom both he and Pilate knew had done no wrong. And what, we ask, was his advantage?

Judas chose the way of the world, and lost his soul in the process. Falling into despair, the eternal night enveloped him. He went out and hanged himself. But what was his profit? Actually, he gained nothing. Nothing of true value or of lasting worth can be accomplished in the work of the Kingdom by devious means. God never works that way. The Gospel narrative in St. Luke tells us that

Judas and the chief priest had agreed: they had agreed in the means to be used, betrayal. Judas could not wash his hand of the means employed, or the person with whom he associated in bringing about the night arrest of the Lord Jesus.

One cannot chose the world as opposed to the Kingdom of heaven and not expect to save his soul unscathed. The spot will not always wash out. And it made no difference whether the chief priest used the means, assented to them, or approved of them. Nor did it matter whether only some advantage or some knowledge was gained. Both voluntarily and intentionally benefited from the means employed, and that forever made them a part of it all. But in the long run, thirty pieces of silver did not really buy very much. It only bought Judas Iscariot; but I have never understood Jesus of Nazareth to have been for sale.

Analysis of Judas Iscariot.

What, then, made Judas do it? Why did Judas Iscariot act as he did? He was not physically compelled to do what he did. He was not legally or morally obligated to betray his Master. St. Augustine makes out a very good case for freedom of the will. Judas acted without compulsion, or out of dire necessity; hence, we are looking for motive. Motive reveals to the world what a man is. What made Judas betray, allegedly, a friend? Why did he forsake the hope and expectation of the ages? What motivated Judas Iscariot to betray the eternal Savior of men?

Generally, it is disappointed ambition, frustrated hopes, and misplaced self-esteem that moves men to act in this manner. Was it not St. Paul who wrote that a man ought not to think too highly of himself? Judas was unrealistic as to his own ability and stature. Holding the purse may have gone to his head. Nevertheless, it appeared that all his treasures were right here on earth with him, rather than in heaven. His concept of the ministry was not one of service and self-sacrifice, but of personal gain and self-aggrandizement. His concept of the Kingdom was of Caesar and earthly, and he remained purely earth-bound.

When Jesus refused the earthly crown, and stated plainly that his Kingdom was not of this world, hope died in Judas Iscariot. All his expectations of glory were in this world. He neither cared for nor sought to understand the realm of spiritual things. The reign of God's love in human hearts had no appeal for him. For Judas Iscariot, all was gone, and the death of Christ on the cross could only have been the end of everything for the purely earth-bound. He was an individual who could never learn to love the Master more than the present world, and subsequently he became the son of perdition. When Judas left the upper room, darkness was already beginning to settle on Holy Week: "He that has hope only in this world is the most miserable of men."

The Transaction and the Individual.

The revelation of the character and motives of Judas, and their outcome, are still instructive for us today. It is vital to all our dealings and all our relationships with other people. A good relationship is not an accident. It just does not happen, or is it stumbled upon. We must create it, support it, and sustain it. It makes no difference whether it is a relationship with our wife, child, or friend. And, in any event, a lasting relationship is not going to be built on mistrust, suspicion, or betrayal. The person one dishonors by his conduct is himself, no one else. With ourselves individually, our family members, and friends, a good relationship must be worked at, and we should do it with perseverance. We will do it with gentleness, inventiveness, and with all the love of our Savior in our hearts.

While our ultimate treasures may be in heaven, here on earth the only thing we really have is each other. When we act, or endeavourer to sustain a good relationship, we will do it out of good motives, out of a pure heart, and with faith unfeigned. Lent is a good time to think about the nature in which we act, and it is always a good time to deepen ties of our relationship with Christ. Our Lord exemplified that service and self-sacrifice were always the way of the Cross. In following the Lord Jesus, it is possible that we may have to assume additional burdens somewhere along the line. It is also possible that we may have to take up a cross here and there, but then we feel certain that the Lord Jesus will love us for that. Even now it can be; it can be our Lord's love and grace kept in our hearts, now and for ever. Amen.

CHAPTER 28

MY TIMES ARE IN GOD'S HANDS

Fourth Sunday in Lent.

As long as we have God as our heavenly Father, we are not alone, regardless of how the outward circumstances may appear. As he worked through his last weeks on earth, our Lord knew that the hour of the cross drew inevitably closer. He also knew that the Father who had sent him would never leave or forsake him. Though the world would do him wrong, the men of the world did not determine his fate, or control his destiny. His life and end were in the hands of God, and greater was he who was with the Lord Jesus, than all the forces of Jewish ecclesiastical control, and all the powers of the imperial might:

> Where will you have us prepare for you to eat the Passover? He said, Go into a city to a certain man, and say to him, The Teacher says, My time is at hand. (Matthew 26:17-18RSV)

When threatened by the wicked queen, Jezebel, Elijah fled, seeking seclusion in the wilderness. Among the clefts of the rocks, he endured the passing of the earthquake, wind, and fire. He was looking for the presence of The Almighty, who appeared after the stilling of the elements. Elijah complained that God's altars were all torn down, all the prophets slain, and that he alone was left alive who served the Lord God. Because of his disappointment, worn condition, and seeming fruitless labor, Elijah was misled by the outward appearances. Not so, said the Lord God. "You are not alone," Said the Lord God. "I have reserved to me seven thousand who have not bowed the knee to Baal."

Though physically, the prophet may have been weary, his spirit spent, and despondent, he was not alone—as apart from other individuals who worshipped God. Nor was he separated from God's presence and help. Elijah was the Lord's prophet, his spokesman and witness on earth, and his mission, as well as his person, fell within God's providence.

In the hurry of our modern society, when pushed and bumped and compelled to move over for those who travel in the fast lane, like the prophet Elijah we will become tired and worn. Our energy will seem to have waned; and though we feel as if we were alone in our struggles, it is not so. The immanence of God is revealed in his living, active, and operative presence throughout the universe. There is no place on earth where we are not in God's presence. Nor would we be separated from God, were to live in the most remote planet in our solar system.

God is behind us, and before us, and about all our ways. In an awareness of his embracing presence, we can always turn to him in our hour of need. This is what we do in the season of lent; we seek to turn toward the presence of God.

My Time, God's Time.

The unveiling of our Lord's humility, and the glory that was to follow upon his sufferings, had well begun. Mary Magdalene, in the house of Simon had anointed Jesus with the precious ointment. She did it, Jesus said, as a preparation for his burial, and then added: "She has done a beautiful thing to me." Those who previously objected to this act held their silence. When the disciples came to the Lord in preparation for the Passover, he told them plainly that his hour was upon him; and that he would be going to the Father through the way of humiliation and suffering. There was no fear, or emotional distress, on the part of the Lord Jesus. When the time of his departure drew near, he prayed as did David in his Psalm: "My Times, O God, are in thy hands."

The events into which Christ was moving were his arrest on false charges, the scattering of his disciples, and Simon Peter following "afar off." There would be the day of scourging and mockery, the crown of thrones, and his derision: they would robed him in the imperial purple, while the Roman soldiers paid mock homage to the Lord Jesus. All these events were still ahead of him.

When the Passover meal was concluded, Jesus and his close disciples went to the garden, a place of seclusion on Mount Olives. Here Christ turned his thoughts to the Father, who for him was ever-present. He was seeking the Father's will and strength for the ordeal to come. In the quiet of the garden, the Lord Jesus prayed, "Not my will, but thine be done." He implied that his life and destiny were in the providential care of God.

Peter, James, and John, three close friends, accompanied the Savior to the Mount of Olives. But having fallen asleep, they were unable to watch and pray with their Master. The crowds had fallen off, and many who once heard him gladly, no longer followed him; and in his hour of need, the three disciples were fast asleep. To the eyes of the world, Christ may have appeared alone, but it was only a moment of seclusion. His time was God's time, and his hour was God's hour. In communion with the Father, he drew deeply from an unending source of strength. The Savior knew it would take more than fortitude to move unflinching through the narrow road that led to the courts of the high priest, the trial, and the cross. He needed the hand of God.

In his book entitled, "Alone," Admiral Byrd wrote how he discovered a hidden source of power to go on in his most desperate hour. He endured five months in the Antarctic, secluded in a hut, buried beneath the polar icecap. At 82 degrees below zero, the cold was extreme, and Byrd was alone. The long winter night settled over the polar icecap. There was no day, only the darkness of the long winter night.

Then, fumes began escaping from his stove, and he realized they were slowly poisoning him. He tried, but was unable to repair the stove. Many times the fumes caused him to fall into unconsciousness. Unable to eat much, or to sleep much, he grew weak, and could only lie in his bunk. Expressing the thoughts that stirred in his mind, he wrote in his dairy:

> The heavens and the stars are held in their course, not one faileth: even the sun with its light will return to the polar cap. (Alone, Admiral Byrd)

Then he added the thought he most wanted to express: "I am not alone." It was a redemptive thought. He had turned his mind inward and upward, like the Lore Jesus in the Garden of Prayer on The Mount of Olives. Admiral Byrd was seeking the strong hand of God in his extremity. This act of mind, springing from the impulse of his soul, released within him strength to endure his Antarctic ordeal. It was strength which he never knew he had; and the energy came from his thoughts of God, and the sense of The Almighty's presence.

Our Lord's Time, Our Time.

When Admiral Byrd turned his thoughts to the providence of God, it was as though he had placed his life in the hands of God: my times, God's hands; my times are in God's hands. From a prison in ancient Rome, St. Paul wrote: "And the Lord stood by me and strengthened me." So found Admiral Byrd, and so have men and women in every generation; and so may we in our own personal lives. When things seem difficult, or grief over loss seems heavy, turning our thoughts to the providence of God and his presence, can be our salvation. When we turn our thoughts to God, we have turned to the ultimate source of power in the universe.

When Admiral Byrd wrote that the heavens and the stars were held in their course, and not one faileth; and that even the sun with its light would return to the polar icecap, he was affirming his belief in God who governs his creation, and provides for its order and fulfillment. Our time is a mode of created existence, and those who acknowledge God's eternal Son, fall within God's providence. Individually, it is our time which is in the hands of God. The Lenten season will give us occasion to think back on the providence of God;

and we will have discovered that his is a benevolent concern for the human race. Regardless of how the outward circumstances may appear, in every situation, as long as we have God as our heavenly Father, we are never alone.

CHAPTER 29

PASSION SUNDAY

THE CROSS AND THE CROWN

The Passion refers to the suffering of Christ, and it includes that period from the time of The Last Supper, to his atonement on the Cross. Scripture affirms that through faith in Christ and in his Passion, we obtain the reward of his righteousness in life and peace.

When she was an infant, nineteen months old, a baby girl was stricken with an illness that left her deaf and blind. To all appearances, it seemed as though she was condemned to a world of darkness and silence for ever. It was not until she was seven years old that her education began. She learned to read with the Braille system and to write with a special typewriter. When she was ten years old, she learned to speak after only one month of instruction. After ten years of study and hard work, she entered Radcliff College and graduated with honors in 1904.

She became an author, writing such titles as; Let Us Have Faith, The Open Door, The World I Live In, and Out Of The Dark. Her life appeared on the silver screen in a play titled, The Miracle Worker. In her lectures, she used the struggles of her life to inspire the handicapped. But before she achieved any measure of success, Helen Keller endured intense study, hard work, and pain. One of her enduring sources of strength came from her religious convictions, which carried Helen Keller to her crown of success and recognition.

The Cross and the Crown.

In historical form, but in simple portrayal, the Church has always presented Christ in the function of his three offices; as a Prophet, Priest, and King. As a Priest, our Lord stands between God and his people as our heavenly mediator. He makes sacrifices, offers prayers and supplications for his people. He leads his people in worship. And in the function of his priestly office, our Lord endured his Passion. The Lenten season is full of opposites, of light and darkness, of self-sacrifice and self-indulgence, of affirmation of faith and denial; but the greatest contrast is that between the Cross and the Crown.

The Cross looms in the foreground, in the background, and on the hill top, and all the while the Crown remains hidden. Yet the glory and diadem at the right hand of God was given our Lord's as a reward for his obedience. In the sequence of events in the weeks of lent, the Cross came before the Crown; and it is also this way in our own personal experience. There is no life without the pain of labor, and no one matures without the struggles of adaptation and growth. Even a lovely rose must endure the sun and the rain to finally emerge in all its beauty.

The Cross and Crown in Human Lives.

It is also true in our own lives that a cross may lead to a crown. When I was fourteen years old, we played with the Cunningham children who lived down the street. One week we would fight, and the next we would play together. One day we were at their house, and their mother ushered us out the back door. My friend, Calvin Cunningham, said, "Mother kicked us out because we were eating all of Uncle Glenn's cinnamon rolls." Uncle Glenn was coming to visit; and he was Glenn Cunningham. As a youth he sustained severe injuries from burns over his body and legs. The best medical opinion thought he would never be able to walk normally again, much less be able to run and play.

But Glenn Cunningham was made of much sterner stuff. He struggled to stand, and then strove to walk, and finally through the agony of tortured skin and muscles he began to run. He refused to surrender to the opinion that he would never walk again. He never ceased his efforts because of pain, and he made his mark in the track and field events of the United States. Before his victories as a runner, Glenn Cunningham struggled with pain and tortured scared tissue, and he overcame. Had he not had his cross, he might not have become the runner he became.

Sometimes, like the Lord Jesus, a cross must be born for others. The life of the writer, Charles Lamb, had all the prospects for success and happiness one could have wished. Yet his life was burdened with trial and sorrow. And although his burden could have been discarded, Charles Lamb covered himself with dignity, fortitude, and honor. What had occurred? When he was twenty years old, his sister, Mary, suffered a fit of insanity and stabbed her mother to death. Subsequently, Charles took the care of Mary as his duty for life.

True, he could have placed her in an asylum for the rest of her days, but he did not do so. She did go there immediately after their mother's death, and back again when she had occasional attacks of madness, but never permanently. Rather, Charles chose to provide a home for them both, and to be her companion and guardian. However, in the process he sacrificed his life for hers. Still, never once did he turn back from his chosen burden. And he cared for Mary without any bitterness of spirit, and without sadness or gloominess. Like the Savior whom he acknowledged, and whom he served, Charles Lamb was a tender and compassionate brother and care giver. Like he who was once crowned with thorns, God crowned Charles Lamb with honor.

Dedicated to the care of his sister and to his profession as a writer, Charles Lamb became great. He developed an attractive and compelling force to his writing, empowered with emotional directness. His character was pervaded with strength grown tender, gentleness, sympathy, understanding, and compassion. Like the Lord Jesus, his silent suffering, his quiet cross, ennobled the man. I am certain that in the eyes of the Lord Jesus, Charles Lamb gained the crown of life.

There are many things to which we can give our lives, and if not all, then surely a part of our lives. None can be more rewarding and more compelling than to give some service for the cause of our Savior's Kingdom. We can do it with gladness, and with the pure joy of giving. That we have done it for the love of our Redeemer should be reward enough for us.

Our Cross, Our Crown.

On Passion Sunday, we are reminded that through faith in Christ—and in his Passion—we obtain of God the reward of righteousness in life and peace. Our faith is grounded in Christ our Lord, and it involves some knowledge of who he was, what he did, and how he did it. This is the simple essence of our Gospel.

How that Christ died for our sins according to the scriptures; And that he was buried, and that he rose again the third day according to the scriptures. (1 Corinthians 15:3-4)

When all is said and done, when all the books have been read, all the theologies written, and all the voices are silent, our standing with our heavenly Father, according to the Christian religion, rest on our commitment to Jesus Christ. We bear his name, sign, seal, and Cross.

We come to worship to sense our Savior's presence among us, and to sense the awakening of our souls to spiritual realities. We come with all our faults, failures, and sins; and all who come to the Lord Jesus, first come to the Christ of the Cross. In following our Savior during season of lent, and the giving of ourselves that we do lovingly for our family and friends—and on occasion the sensitive emotions we endure—through the grace of our Lord Jesus Christ, all add strength, beauty, and depth to our existence. It is to the eternal testimony of the Christian experience, that one's character can be pervaded with strength grown tender, which becomes gentleness.

All the anxieties of this world can vanish like a whiff of smoke on the soft spring breeze. We will have gained sympathy, understanding, and compassion for those less fortunate than we. We can accept the fact, and live with the reality, that a cross must come before our crown.

CHAPTER 30

PALM SUNDAY

REJECTING AND RECEIVING

When the Lord Jesus came into the city of Jerusalem on Palm Sunday, the entire population seemed caught up in the occasion of the moment. They shouted, "Hosanna, blessed is he that cometh in the name of the Most High." But scarcely a week later, when Christ stood in Pilate's court, he stood alone. He had become a stone of decision, and when presented before the crowd on the first Good Friday, he was a stumbling-block. Although the people had shouted his praises on Palm Sunday, the end of our Lord's visit to the city came out as an evil thing. They turned away from the Lord Jesus.

Even today, we can do one of two things with this strange and wonderful prophet of Nazareth; and the Lenten season is the time when we prepare to make our decision. Like the multitude of that far distant past, we can either reject him as Lord—or we can chose to receive him, together with his grace and love. It must have been with a heavy heart that John wrote in his Gospel: "He came unto his own, and his own received him not" (John 1:11). But in the wonder and simplicity of God's dealings with men, to "as many as received him, to them he gave the power to become the sons of God" (John 1:12).

Jesus was Rejected Then.

When Jesus walked this earth, his followers came to embrace him as their Lord. But the vast majority of the people declined the Savior's invitation to enter the Kingdom of God. We would ask: "Who rejected Jesus? Who declined his gracious invitation to come into the Kingdom of Heaven?" We would naturally think that Jesus was rebuffed by strangers, or by those who never heard what the prophets had written about him. We would think that the Gentiles who envied and suspected the Jews were the ones that discarded him as just another strange prophet come out of the wilderness. Perhaps, we would like to believe that the Samaritans, who hated the Jews and had no dealings with them, were the first to repudiate the man of sorrows. But such was not the case. It was his own people who by and large refused to have anything to do with Jesus of Nazareth.

Viewed from the background of the Christian centuries, we can't imagine how any one who heard Jesus speak, or saw him minister to the sick and blind could have repudiated the Savior. But that was exactly what occurred. Did not our Lord say, "Blessed are they who have not seen, yet believe?" Cast out of the temple, at first, by the religious leaders, he was also cast aside by the common people in favor of a condemned criminal. All turned from him at the end, except his disciples and the women who tended the Savior's needs.

We are interested in knowing how those ancient people went about rejecting Jesus. There were those who passed over Jesus by refusing to hear him. Once, when Jesus healed a man, everyone became startled. The man had been mad, and Jesus brought him back to sanity. Someone or something startled a herd of swine so that they ran over a cliff into the water and were destroyed. The consensus of opinion was that Jesus was the kind of man who could cause trouble. They refused to suffer the Lord Jesus to remain in their locality. They would not give him so much as a hearing. They told him to get in a boat and go back to where he came from. They rejected Jesus by refusing to hear his message.

There were those who, while they may have heard what Jesus had to say, rejected him by refusing to believe. If we do not believe, we certainly are not going to do anything about what we have heard.

Jesus said that we should not be hearers only, but also doers of his words. There was the outright rejection of Jesus by those who refused to give him standing among the prophets. Others rejected him by having nails driven through his hands and feet, and leaving him on the Cross to die in agony. But by whatever means employed, one rejection was as final as any other.

Why did all those people reject Jesus? What reason prompted them to rebuff the Christ of God? Surely, it had more to do than with the way he combed his hair or wore his clothes. It had nothing to do with his physical appearance. It was more than likely that his simple life was a constant reproach to all of them. When Christ kept asking questions which they refused to answer; when Jesus opposed the religious leaders, telling them that true faith and an honest heart counted more in the sight of God than a loud prayer or a big contribution to the treasury, they rejected him. And when Jesus drove the money changers out of the temple, his death was sealed. Rejection turned to hatred, and their hatred could only be appeased by the Savior's death.

If people had accepted Jesus and his teaching, they would have had to change their way of life. Changing their way of life entailed too much effort. If the priest had authenticated Christ's message, they would have had to change their way of practicing their religion, and this would have cost them too much money. They all desired to serve at least two masters, perhaps more. Rejecting Jesus avoided all the unpleasantness, and all the startling things that could have happened to them, had they chosen to follow him.

He is Rejected Today.

While men can no longer drive nails through Christ's hands and feet today, they still reject Christ as Lord. We live in an age we like to think as modern. We believe we are highly cultured and moderately civilized. We pride ourselves in that we are not hampered by gross superstitions. We would like to believe we have been trained in the modern ways of thinking. And we would like to base our beliefs, if we have any, on reason and scientific fact. The increase of knowledge within the past three decades alone has been overwhelming. We have received so many facts, and from so many fields of science, and in so short a time, that our minds and imaginations can hardly contain them all. Questions, and doubts, may arise because of the new ideas, which all this knowledge implies. And hence, we may think that ideas have arisen, which stand in opposition to our ancient faith in Christ Jesus.

Being human, and possessed with a creative mind, some individuals may question the basic Christian beliefs on which our faith is founded. Questions follow questions concerning the Christian way of life, faith in God; and faith in the grace of our Lord Jesus Christ. And it is entirely possible that a strange and alien perplexity may have arisen in our minds. And in the wistfulness of blurred eyes, we may be practicing a refined rejection of the Lord Jesus Christ.

How do we reject Jesus today? We tend to slight him as our Redeemer. We continue going our own indifferent ways. Yet, we inherently recognize the good qualities in the Christian religion. And we do not want our children to grow up into complete pagans. Still, we feel that we are more than capable of making our own way in the world. And I will be the first to admit that there is a way that "seemeth right in a man's eyes." But what shall be the end thereof? We do not even know what a day may bring forth, yet we persist in rejecting Jesus by going our own way without him. We have excluded the Master by not acknowledging him fully as Savior and Lord. We set him aside, when we make our most important decisions. We repudiate him, when we feel ashamed to take him with us into our office, or to the home of a friend. There are hundreds of ways in which we may renounce the Lord Jesus, however refined each may be.

And why do we reject Jesus today? The Lenten season is a good time to ask this question. Is it because we believe that Christ, and all he stands for runs counter to modern thinking? I doubt this. We may be perplexed, but surely we are not mad. We know what is good and right when we see it. We admire a noble character, a pure heart, and a person who endeavors to follow the Master as best as he can. We know that these individuals have been the lights of every darkened era of our history.

We hesitate to entertain Jesus because we know that he demands singleness of purpose. If we suffer him to lead and teach us, we will no longer go our own indifferent ways. Perhaps, we believe that some of the joys of life may be curtailed, if we choose to follow him. We do not wish to follow in what we may have construed as a restricted mode of livng. We desire to taste all of life; we want to drink the whole of it. We know that Jesus will be Lord of all, or not at all. So we decline to accept him on this basis.

Christ Can Always be Received.

The Church, and all who are a part of her, prepares during the season of lent to receive the Christ, who offered himself up for the life of the world. We prepare for Christ, who once again reminds us of the hope of Easter morning. The time of the lengthening of days brings to light our Lord's steadfastness in the presence of denial, rejection, and betrayal. This occurred two thousand years ago, when Christ first presented himself to the world. Once again, in lent, by the solemnity of the season, we are made aware that Jesus Christ stands ready to be received by all who will admit him. This is the wonder and mystery of his grace: Christ can always be received as Savior and Lord.

We may ask ourselves, "How can our Lord offer himself to us anew, after the crucifixion, and after repeated rejections by the children of men?" How? Christ offers himself anew because God will make known his love and mercy to every generation. We can receive Christ by hearing him and believing on his Gospel. Belief and faith are acts of the intellect. They are the response of heart and mind to our Lord's summons: "Blessed are they which do hunger and thirst after righteousness...for they shall be filled...I am the bread of life; he that cometh unto me shall never hunger, and he that believeth on me shall never thirst." Christ becomes our Redeemer, when hearing and believing, we allow his love and Spirit to reside in us.

What happens when Jesus is received? To those who receive him, he gives the power to become the sons and daughters of God. He removes the misty perplexity from blurred eyes, and enables one to move into the spiritual realities of his grace and glory. And however much knowledge may have advanced in all fields of human endeavor, we have not outgrown our need of God's grace, mercy, and love. This outpouring of grace, God manifested and gave to us in Christ Jesus our Lord. All who trust the final destiny of their lives to Christ Jesus, and all who desire to see in Jesus the visible image of the Father; can embrace him as their Lord. In spite of past rejections, despite previous exclusions of his influence by us, our Redeemer ever stands at the door of humanity's heart, awaiting the call of spirit to spirit.

Whatever our condition, if we wish to receive him, Jesus will come in and sup with us, and we with him. With a child, a parent, or grand-parent, this gentle Jesus, meek and mile, is always ready to be received. During the Lenten season, we may prepare to receive and follow this wonderful Savior of men. The season of lent was preserved for the Church of Jesus Christ for just this reason: that our spiritual life be renewed, strengthened, and preserved unto the day of his appearing. This is the Savior whom I leave with you on this occasion: he who is always ready to be received through simple faith in believing hearts. And when we do this: believe in him; trust in him, he becomes our Savior and Lord. This is the gift of God's grace to us during the season of Lent. We have but to receive.

CHAPTER 31

MAUNDY THURSDAY
(Communion)

I HAVE PRAYED FOR YOU

Thursday in Holy Week is known as Maundy Thursday. In our communion services held on this day, we commemorate our Lord's last hour with his disciples. We come to restore our souls in worship, and to strengthen our religious convictions. We have experienced periods, when it seemed as though we were in constant need of encouragement. But then, who has never had moments of weakness? Whose faith has never faltered? Even great men in the affairs of nations and religious movements have questioned the certainty of their position.

John the Baptist sent two of his disciples to inquire whether the Lord Jesus came as the appointed one, or should he look for another? Christ understood and sympathized with the Baptist. He knew that the desert wrought prophet had acute spiritual perception; and in a simple review of his ministry, the Lord Jesus answered John's inquiry:

> Go tell John what you have seen and heard; the blind receive their sight, the lame walk, lepers are cleansed, and the deaf hear, and the dead are raised up, and the poor have the good news preached to them. (Luke 7:22RSV)

The grace of our Lord's ministry bore witness that God was with him. And it is always a true sign of the Kingdom, when the poor have the Gospel preached to them. John the Baptist inquired no more.

I Have Prayed for You.

Though all may falter because we are human, through our Lord's intercession and presence of the Spirit, we may be strengthened and encouraged in our faith. This was confirmed on that first Maundy Thursday Communion of long ago. The Last Supper was over, and the Lord Jesus informed his disciples that he was betrayed. Immediately they began to question one another about this matter. They also questioned who among them would be most prominent. Probably Peter expressed his opinion more forcefully. And the Savior said to him.

> Simon, Simon, behold Satan demanded to have you, that he might sift you as wheat, but I have prayed for you that your faith may not fail; and when you have turned again, strengthen your brethren. (Luke 22:31-32)

This sacrament, in which we share the bread and wine, does more than mirror out Lord's life and mission. It is also the token and pledge of our Savior's mediatorial office, of his intercession on behalf of those who have confessed him as God's Redeemer. One way in which Christ intercedes for us is by his prayer for our spiritual well-being. He went to the cross for us, and can plead the blood of his atonement. In his mediatorial office, the Lord Jesus is our advocate with the Father.

The Lord Jesus warned Peter. He tried to make him aware of what lay in the immediate future. Christ himself would be arrested and the disciples scattered. Outside, beyond the upper room, a hostile world waited for them with no good purpose. That very night, Simon Peter faltered. He denied his Master three times, and then went out into the darkness and wept bitterly at his failure. Yet, in the grace that Simon Peter had received from the Lord Jesus, he would be turned again. Not because Peter was the largest or most forceful of the disciples, but because Christ had prayed for him. Within the composition of our own bodies, we have the same feelings, strengths, and weaknesses as did Simon Peter. And during the season of lent, our spiritual inclination is also like that of Simon Peter's: we are subject to spiritual mood swings.

Fortunately, it does not matter that we suffer from mood swings, that on occasion we commit a fault, and that our religious life, more often than not, may seem listless and inert. No one lives on an elevated spiritual plane day in and day out. And we all confess that we would like more depth and more assurance in our religious expression. This is why we have turned aside on Maundy Thursday, to worship, to be strengthened by this sacrament of Holy Communion, and to be confirmed in our deep religious convictions. Nothing can be more invigorating for us in these matters, than the knowledge that Christ the Lord, the Redeemer come from the threshold of heaven, has prayed for us. When Christ prayed for his disciples, he added these words to that prayer.

> I do not pray for these only, but also for all who believe in me through their word, that they all be one. (John 17:20)

Prayer was an every day thing with the Lord Jesus, and it ought to be common to men and women who seek his presence. Prayer is an impulse stemming from our soul and the interpreter of our religious feelings. It is an act of worship. And as prayer is offered to our heavenly Father from a sincere heart and an honest faith, it becomes an up-lifting spiritual experience. When we make ready to take the elements of bread and wine into our bodies, we are instructed in Scripture to look within ourselves. Before God, no outward display can hide the true nature of things, however presentable the appearance. And he whom we seek to remember in the sacrament of Holy Communion, searches the thoughts of the heart and the imaginations of the mind. Our Lord's prayer aids in keeping our faith from failing, because he is the source of our spiritual life. Our own prayers cause us to look within, to unite with the Lord Jesus, as we express the thoughts that come from the impulse of our soul.

I Will not Leave You Desolate.

During that first Maundy evening communion service, the Savior spoke to his immediate followers about the coming events of Holy Week. He told them they would be disturbed, and even shaken severely by the rapid sequence of the drama unfolding before them: "You will be scattered...and will leave me alone; yet I am not alone, for the Father is with me" (John 16:32RSV). Regardless of how the disciples reacted under the pressure of Christ's arrest, the trial, and the Cross, the Savior passed through all these incidents unmoved. The disciples were fearful, hesitant, and then dispersed. And as far as his group of close followers was concerned, they left Jesus to himself to suffer through the ordeal alone. Yet, the Christ of God had affirmed before hand that in spite of how things seemed to the world at large, he was not alone, for God was with him. The sense of the Father's presence never left him; and God's presence gave our Lord's life and mission the quality of eternity.

Having identified with us in his body, Christ knew how the feeling of loneliness might affect us. He not only made intercession for us, he also promised not to leave us alone, when friends might leave us, when we must travel unaccompanied, or when left to ourselves to make an important decision: "I will not leave you desolate: I will come to you" (John 14:18RSV). Christ would not leave his people to be overwhelmed by the feeling that he had forsaken them, when they might be most in need of their Savior's presence.

Everywhere the disciples went in the discharge of their great commission, no matter how far they might be separated from family and friends, in the far and lonely reaches of the empire, they took their faith with them. And the experience of the fellowship in the upper room went with them. In the budding gathering of new believers, they celebrated the sacrament of Holy Communion, and the sacrament brought home to them in a very real way an awareness of their Savior's presence. He came to them in all the dynamic force and power of his resurrection.

This we sense in the service of the consecrated elements of bread and wine. We come to hear the Savior's words: "This is my body which was given for you...This cup is the new covenant in my blood which is shed for many, for the remission of sins...I will not leave you desolate: in this hour of worship, in the celebration of the sacrament, I will come to you." And Christ comes to us as he came to his disciples, with all the dynamic force and spiritual power of his resurrection to confirm our belief in him, to revive our souls, and to strengthen our spiritual life.

I Will Send the Counselor.

How would our Lord come to his disciples after he had gone to be with the Father? And how would his presence be with them? He would be with them in the presence and power of the Holy Spirit.

> The Counselor...whom I shall send to you from the Father, even the Spirit of truth, who proceeds from the Father, he will bear witness of me. (John 1:26RSV)

In the days immediately prior to Easter Sunday, throughout the nation, in thousands of churches, special services are held on Maundy Thursday, Good Friday, and Holy Saturday. These services confirm the ancient tradition, that in the moving events of the Lenten season, the Spirit of the Most High draws near. The words of our Lord Jesus about the Counselor bearing witness, attest to the greatest reality of the Christian Religion—*the presence of God, in his Spirit, with his people.* The Spirit residing in the heart gives evidence of the Savior's coming. It corroborates the presence of Christ with his Church, and with the believer individually.

It is true, that on occasion we sense a weakness, ineffectiveness in the impulse of our religious life. It is a thing common to human beings. We ought not to be startled, or even surprised. We all run on the tide of life, on the ebb and flow of our spiritual life. It does not mean that we have fallen from grace, only that we are spent, and that the inner flame of our conviction must be rekindled. Through the word and the sacrament, in the remembrance of our Lord's prayer for us—in the soft touch of the Spirit on our souls bearing witness to God's presence—the strength of our religious convictions will return. Like with the incoming tide, the strength of our religious convictions returns slowly, softly, during the season of lent.

CHAPTER 32

GOOD FRIDAY

NE PLUS ULTRA

People everywhere have expressed the opinion that they are angry, confused, and fed up with the broken promises of big government, which itself is seemingly gripped in the vice of futility and despair. Can the average person really believe that the state will save him, redeem his soul from destruction, and fulfill the destiny of his life? One respondent to a weekly news magazine recently complained: "We have been left with nothing to believe in."

Modern Americans appear like the peoples of ancient times who looked for peace and safety; and instead found a time of anguish for their souls. We deceive ourselves, if we search for light and hope in each new administration. Is it not true, that the dreams and visions of the "Great Society," have faded away beyond all possibility of retrieving? Bilingual education is not going to solve our most pressing problems, nor will a multiplicity of new programs answer the most urgent need of the human soul. This is not to say that we have forgotten the needs of the fatherless, the poor, the disabled, and care for the widows of him who shall have born the battle.

They Turned the People Against Him.

On Good Friday, the people were confused, fed up, and angry. The chief priests and scribes had convinced them that they had been played with, made sport of, and betrayed. The newly come prophet, Jesus of Nazareth, had pulled at their heartstrings, aroused their emotions, while appealing to their hopes and dreams for a better world. This Son of man from Galilee, who stood between the accusing scribes and the Roman Procurator, hardly answered a word. The mob of the chief priests with its instigators, the base fellows among them who had sold themselves for greed, now stirred up the multitude. They evoked their feelings of anger, and urged them to cry out for vengeance.

The Son of man's crucifixion without the gates of the city, up that hill of gloom called Calvary, making an end of him there, was the only thing that appeased the mad fury of the mob. The religious authorities had done their work well. They had engaged Judas to arrange for Jesus' arrest, had manipulated the administration of justice and the trial, and had worked the multitude into the frenzy of revenge.

Through imperial indifference, the envy of an offended priesthood, and the perversity of the people, Jesus Christ was condemned to die—though he had done no wrong. And while rejected of men, he was chosen and precious in God's sight. From his time in history, looking ahead into the prophetic future, Isaiah, son of Amos, wrote: "He was despised and rejected of men; a man of sorrows and acquainted with grief" (Isaiah 53:3RSV).

He had Done no Wrong.

The end of our Lord's earthly ministry on the Cross of Good Friday was a heroic tragedy; and in the nobility of his character, the Lord Jesus did not succumb to retaliating in kind to the mocking crowd beneath the Cross. His last hours were far above the concept of ordinary suffering, and because he had done no wrong, his suffering proved to be redemptive in the sight of God the Father. Not having done wrong, why then was Jesus condemned? The Christ of God died because of his religious concepts, which were embodied in the Gospel he preached. He went up the hill of Calvary because he was receptive to sinners. They drove nails through his hands and feet because he healed on the Sabbath and had raised the daughter of Jairus from the sleep of death.

The religious authorities brought Christ to trial, because he preached grace so freely, that he threw open wide the doors of the Kingdom of heaven to whosoever might come. Our Lord was hated by the self-righteous scribes because he was sympathetic, understanding, and forgiving to the woman taken in adultery; and the Lord Jesus was lifted up on the Cross because he cast aside the entire package of their traditions in directing the affection of love to God and to one's neighbor. Because the grace of God worked through Jesus to heal the sick, the religious authorities hated him; and as empowered by the Spirit of God, when he confessed his authority to forgive sins, the hatred of the chief priests and scribes turned to murder and they crucified him.

We can scarcely imagine anyone today hating the Lord Jesus simply because of the Gospel he preached, or because his demeanor was characterized by gentleness and meekness. Since he confessed that he had not come to mingle with the righteous, but to minister the grace of God to ordinary, every day sinners, would we classify him as guilty by association? Because we may be unable to understand how Jesus could open the eyes of the blind and make the lame walk, would we accuse him of working his miracles of healing through the powers of darkness?

It is possible that those individuals responsible for the crucifixion had nothing left to believe in. Was it because they no longer believed—in spiritual realities or in the redemption of the soul, or in the forgiveness of sins and the resurrection of the body—that they forced the Lord Jesus to ascend Calvary? Peace, love, truth, faith, hope, and joy in the Holy Spirit, there is no law against these things. Not having committed a crime against the state, or done an injury to an individual, the Lord Jesus was crucified for his religious convictions and practice, and for the Gospel of grace he preached.

Who has Believed Our Report?

> Who has believed what we have heard? And to whom has the arm of the Lord been revealed. (Isaiah 53:9RSV)

The opposition to our Lord's ministry, by Good Friday, had solidified because he was seen as one estranged from the order of Aaron and the Levitical priesthood. Jesus did not fall within their concept of what the anointed one and Redeemer of Israel might be. Isaiah said that this was he, The Suffering Servant, come from the Father, who would make many righteous because he will have born their iniquities. But those, to whom Jesus came directly, did not believe the words of the prophet. Nor did they believe when the promised Redeemer visited their cities, mingled with the people, and drew his illustrations about the Kingdom of heaven from the country side.

The prophet Isaiah was compelled to ask, "Who has believed our preaching," our Gospel, our Redeemer come to fulfill the promise made to the fathers in times long since past. This was he who had promised to bring them living water; and they had only to believe and nothing more. But they would not. Since the Redeemer's advent was foretold, what happened that they were unable to believe on him? The reason was that because the Lord Jesus did not appear in their accepted religious pattern, they refused to accept him. Having refused to accept Jesus of Nazareth as the promised Messiah, they would never believe.

Is it possible that we, and others like us, may be troubled with the same difficulty in accepting a Redeemer who comes in the spirit of meekness and gentleness? Yes, this may be true. It is very possible that during the Lenten season, the Savior may approach us individually in ways and form that we do not anticipate, and because of this we will be unaware of his presence. Jesus may attempt to speak to us through the affections and kindness of another human being; and because of our structured mental disposition, we may not recognize him. We may lack the receptivity of heart to welcome the Spirit's touch upon our lives, because a certain type of religious experience has not occurred with us; and that will pose an obstacle to our believing. And yet, the miracle of God's grace and the wonder of his love have been revealed to us.

We may have a mental barrier in accepting what Christ claimed to be, and what he has promised to effect in our souls, and in our relationship with God. The chief priests and scribes were unable to accept the Lord Jesus as he presented himself to the people of his time—as the one who left the glory that he had with the Father and assumed human form. They could not admit to themselves that Christ came in the Spirit and power of the divine to reveal the character and purpose of God, and with the ability to heal the sick and the authority to forgive sins. How near impossible it appears for the proud, the self-righteous, and the powerful to believe that all they have to do is come, approach the Christ of the Cross, and look. The God-man on the Cross is the heroic Redeemer of men; and because of his exceptional service to mankind, he was chosen and precious in God's sight.

Ne Plus Ultra.

Simon peter wrote in his first epistle:

Come to him, to that living stone, rejected by men but in God's sight chosen and precious; and like living stones be yourselves built into a spiritual house. (1 Peter 2:4RSV)

Through a worldly tribunal where justice faltered, the Lord Jesus was condemned. Because Christ came with a Spirit and grace unknown to the religious authorities of his day, they rejected him. And because the people allowed themselves to be swayed and frustrated in their earthly expectations, the Christ of God was crucified on Good Friday. The Cross of our Lord Jesus, lifted up on Good Friday, marked the ultimate separation from all worldly ambitions, and from all the disappointments we permit to drag down the aspirations of the soul. The Cross is also the final rejection of the Lord Jesus by a world of men insensitive to things unseen, who were divorced in their thinking from the way and means God employed to reach the human heart.

In all the seasons of the Church year and especially in the season of lent, there is "Ne Plus Ultra:" there is nothing beyond the Cross for the remission of sins, the cleansing of the soul, and turning to the Lord Jesus. "Ne Plus Ultra" means there is nothing beyond—

nothing else can do for the human soul what Christ in his Atonement has done.

When the Lord God gave us the Christ of the Cross, he gave us a saving and atoning Christ, and God gave us his all. For those who would know the Lord God more intimately, it is immaterial that others have not accepted the Savior's invitation. Our Lord's invitation is still extended to you and to your posterity for ever. Come to that living Stone, chosen and precious in God's sight. He is the foundation of the Church, the source of her inner being. And it is his Spirit and grace that will nurture and encourage your spiritual life. There is "Ne Plus Ultra" beyond the Christ of the Cross.

CHAPTER 33

EASTER SUNDAY

SUNSET-SUNRISE

On the first Easter Sunday, when Mary Magdalene came to the tomb seeking her Lord, she paused, and stood there weeping. They had taken away her Lord and she did not know where she might find him. Although Mary failed to recognize him, Jesus was standing there by her side all the time. The Savior appeared to her in a form other than that which she had known, and she failed to perceive him standing by her side. Then Jesus called her by name, "Mary." And, suddenly, by the inflection of his voice, she knew him. "Master," was all she could say in awe and wonder. Mary Magdalene had found her risen and living Lord.

A Risen and Living Lord.

We do not pay homage to a cross, nor do we look back on an empty tomb. A risen and living Lord is the triumphant hall mark of the Christian religion, the glory and expectation of the Church. On Easter Sunday, we commemorate the resurrection of our Lord Jesus Christ. The apostle Paul, when writing to the church in Corinth, placed the certainty—and the ground of all Christian believing—on the reality of our Savior's resurrection. His words are simple and direct.

> For I delivered unto you first of all that which I also received, how that Christ died for our sins according to the scriptures: And that he was buried, and that he rose again the third day according to the scriptures. (1 Corinthians 15:3-4)...
>
> And if Christ be not risen, then is our preaching vain, and your faith is also vain. (1 Corinthians 15:14)

The preceding of what the apostle proclaimed—his entire Gospel of grace, forgiveness, a new spiritual life, the Lordship of Jesus, and immortality were based on his belief that Christ died for our sins according to the Scriptures; and that he rose again on the third day according to the Scriptures. He then added; and if Christ be not risen, all is vain. Vain means futile, worthless, empty, and of no real value. All Paul's labor as the apostle to the Gentiles who evangelized an empire would be worthless. All his suffering, privation, and anguish of soul would be futile. Even Paul's death as an early martyr for the cause he embraced would have been vain were not Christ risen. His epistles would be no more than words of inspirational writing, rather than the unfolding of the revelation of Jesus Christ. And the faith of those whom his mission had turned to the Lord Jesus would have been of no real value. But the history of the Christian religion has proven otherwise. Faith in the crucified and risen Christ has refused to die.

Faith in Christ refused to die, because faith in him had been transformed and transfigured after the power of an endless life, when God wrought again the Lord Jesus from the dead. It was the risen Lord whom St. Paul encountered in his conversion experience on the lonely road to Damascus. It is the Spirit of our living Lord that moves every heart, that touches every soul, and turns men and women to the saving and atoning Christ of the cross. Our belief in immortality is implied in the sovereignty of God—and certified in our Lord's resurrection.

We are aware that the Christ of the Cross has never appealed to an age of sophistication, or to an intellectual slant of the mind hostile to a holy God and a pure church. From the cross we move to our risen Lord. Still, all who would be numbered among the sons and daughters of God must first know the Christ of the cross. To come to the Father, we must accept the way of God's appointing; and that way leads to the cross; and from there to a risen and living Lord. A living Lord is the end of all that occurred on Easter morning.

Sunset-Sunrise.

While it is true that there will be an end to our lives on earth, it is also true that we shall awaken to a beautiful sunrise. All through the first Lenten season Mary's love was the emblem of our Lord's resurrection. While the disciples' eyes and minds were still on the Savior's death and the end of a beautiful dream, Mary Magdalene had seen and conversed with her risen Lord. The Savior's form was not recognized by her, when she first saw him. She supposed him to be someone else, and appealed to him for assistance in finding her Lord. Yet, Jesus was very close to her all the time. But for a moment, the spiritual sensitivity of her soul had not awakened to his presence. But she knew her Master's voice, and when Jesus called her by name, she knew it was he. Knowledge of his presence moved Mary's soul, called out her heart, and overwhelmed her.

But for the disciples, there was still gloom and despair. The change in their outlook began when two of them were on their way to Emmaus. Their voices had given expression to their thoughts. The conversation they were holding with each other was about Jesus of Nazareth, a mighty prophet in deed and word before God and all the people. He had been condemned to death by the authorities, and heaviness had fallen on their souls. Their hopes were fading into the sunset, for they added: "We trusted that it had been he which should have redeemed Israel" (Luke 24:21).

They were explaining these things to the risen Lord who had drawn near to them as they walked along the way. But like Mary, at first, they eyes were holden and they did not recognize Jesus. Yet, as they talked with this one who had joined them on the way, it were as though their hearts burned within them. Unknown to these two disciples, they had sensed the presence of the divine, as when spirit to spirit speak. And, as though hope refused to die with the unrecognized Jesus so near, they said: "and this is the third day since this happened." The sun had already set, and night was falling.

Not wanting to part from this supposed stranger, they bade him come in and sup with them. He consented and broke bread with them at their table. And as if awakened from a dream, immediately, in the breaking of the bread, they knew him. They saw his grace and glory. Though the night outside had now completely fallen, Jesus Christ had changed the sunset in their hearts to sunrise of their souls. Faith, hope, and love once again soared on the wings of the Spirit: "in the sure and certain hope of the resurrection unto eternal life, through Jesus Christ our Lord." They were no longer disillusioned.

Sunrise: Heroic Optimism.

When the realization of what occurred on the first Easter morning finally came home to the disciples, it released within them a heroic optimism in their Lord and in their faith.

Into a dark tremendous Sea of Cloud,
It is but for a time: I press God's lamp
Close to my breast: its splendor soon or late
Will pierce the gloom: I shall emerge one day.

Robert Browning wrote that. He also wrote, "Sun-Trader, I believe in God and trust." Robert Browning appeared as a man for whom disillusion was impossible. No defeat could overwhelm the poet who wrote: "I was ever a fighter." His trust in God enabled him to display a heroic optimism he never permitted to die. He expressed the opinion that the average man lives, and must move on the belief that life is worth living; and that it is so from one day to the next. Without faith, it is possible that life may cease for many men and women. All our faults, failures, and sins are only shadows. And through the wonder of Easter morning, life holds the promise of immortality.

"I was ever a fighter," Browning wrote. "I have fought the good fight," wrote St. Paul to Timothy. So said the Apostolic Fathers. So said the Protestant Reformers, when darkness overshadowed the earth. And once again the light of the simple Gospel of grace, with all the power and glory of the resurrection, burst through the gloom and drove back the darkness. The night shall be as the day, for Jesus Christ has changed sunset to sunrise. Even in the loss of death, when we lay a loved one to rest, we do so in the sure and certain hope of the resurrection unto eternal life, through Jesus Christ our Lord. Jesus Christ has changed sunset to sunrise, and he has done so for ever. A-men.

[End]